CW00361565

Windows 98 explained

BOOKS AVAILABLE

By both authors:

BP327 DOS one step at a time
BP337 A Concise User's Guide to Lotus 1-2-3 for Windows
BP341 MS-DOS explained
BP346 Programming in Visual Basic for Windows
BP352 Excel 5 explained
BP362 Access one step at a time
BP372 CA-SuperCalc for Windows explained
BP387 Windows one step at a time
BP388 Why not personalise your PC
BP399 Windows 95 one step at a time*
BP400 Windows 95 explained
BP402 MS Office one step at a time
BP405 MS Works for Windows 95 explained
BP406 MS Word 95 explained
BP407 Excel 95 explained
BP408 Access 95 one step at a time
BP409 MS Office 95 one step at a time
BP415 Using Netscape on the Internet*
BP419 Using Microsoft Explorer on the Internet*
BP420 E-mail on the Internet*
BP426 MS-Office 97 explained
BP428 MS-Word 97 explained
BP429 MS-Excel 97 explained
BP430 MS-Access 97 one step at a time
BP433 Your own Web site on the Internet
BP448 Lotus SmartSuite 97 explained
BP456 Windows 98 explained*

By Noel Kantaris:

BP258 Learning to Program in C
BP259 A Concise Introduction to UNIX*
BP284 Programming in QuickBASIC
BP325 A Concise User's Guide to Windows 3.1

Windows 98 explained

by

N. Kantaris
and
P.R.M. Oliver

BERNARD BABANI (publishing) LTD.
THE GRAMPIANS
SHEPHERDS BUSH ROAD
LONDON W6 7NF
ENGLAND

PLEASE NOTE

Although every care has been taken with the production of this book to ensure that any projects, designs, modifications and/or programs, etc., contained herewith, operate in a correct and safe manner and also that any components specified are normally available in Great Britain, the Publishers and Author(s) do not accept responsibility in any way for the failure (including fault in design) of any project, design, modification or program to work correctly or to cause damage to any equipment that it may be connected to or used in conjunction with, or in respect of any other damage or injury that may be so caused, nor do the Publishers accept responsibility in any way for the failure to obtain specified components.

Notice is also given that if equipment that is still under warranty is modified in any way or used or connected with home-built equipment then that warranty may be void.

© 1998 BERNARD BABANI (publishing) LTD

First Published - September 1998

British Library Cataloguing in Publication Data:

A catalogue record for this book is available from the
British Library

ISBN 0 85934 456 8

Cover Design by Gregor Arthur
Cover illustration by Adam Willis
Printed and Bound in Great Britain by Cox & Wyman Ltd, Reading

PREFACE

Microsoft produced the first version of Windows in 1983 as a graphical extension to its Disc Operating System (MS-DOS). However, it was not a great success because, being DOS based, it was confined to the DOS memory limit of 1MB of RAM. Mind you, at that time, not many PCs had that much memory!

In 1987, an Intel 386 processor specific version of Windows was brought out that was able to run in multiple 'virtual 8086' mode, but Windows applications were still unable to use any extended memory above the 1MB. In 1990, however, Windows version 3.0 solved this problem and became a huge success.

Two years later, the much needed update, Windows version 3.1, was released in April 1992 to fix most of the program bugs in version 3.0. The horrendous and frequent 'Unrecoverable Application Error' message became a thing of the past. Windows for Workgroups 3.1, followed in October 1992, and started to give the program the power to control small networked groups of computers. This was strengthened in October 1993 with the 3.11 release, which included 32-bit file management and more networking support.

Then came an almost three year wait for Windows 95, a 32-bit operating system in its own right. It was the first 'non-specialist' operating system to make full use of the 32-bit features of the then available range of Intel processor chips. Microsoft had also put a lot of effort into this system to make it compatible with almost all existing Windows and MS-DOS based applications. This was obviously necessary, but it meant that parts of Windows 95 were still only 16-bit in operation.

Finally in June 1998, we saw the launch of Windows 98, the long awaited refined upgrade to Windows 95, which runs faster, crashes less frequently, supports a host of new technologies, such as Digital Video Disc for storing high quality digital video on PCs, improved MMX multimedia, and is year 2000 compliant.

Windows 98 Recommendations:

You might have read in an article in The Sunday Times (9/8/98) that a British software house, Prove It 2000, reported that they had found a potentially damaging date bug in Windows 98 Standard edition. According to the article, setting the PC's clock to just 30 seconds before any year's end, and allowing the clock to run over to the new year, caused the PC's date to jump either 2 days forward, or 1 day backwards.

We have tried to simulate the reported error, but without any success. Nevertheless, this could be an error which is system dependant, and Microsoft is examining the code of the program that unearthed the reported bug. While this bug, if indeed it exists, could become inconvenient or even damaging to certain applications users, we are sure that Microsoft will soon report on it, and if necessary post a fix on their Web site. If you find that your system is affected by such a bug, and you are connected to the Internet, then refer to the penultimate section in Chapter 8 where we tell you how to use the Windows Update utility to obtain such a fix easily and quickly.

One of the well publicised new feature in Windows 98 is the rapid shutdown procedure. This feature, while desirable, has caused Windows 98 to hang several times at shutdown, with the result that we had to switch off the power to our PC. This, of course, caused Windows to scan our hard disc for errors the very next time our system was switched on. If you encounter a similar problem, then refer to the last section in Chapter 8 where we tell you how to cure it completely.

If you like to speed up both the startup and shutdown procedures of Windows 98 and be in total control of your system, then look up the penultimate section of Chapter 9 where we tell you how to do it.

Finally, having used Windows 98 solidly every day for the past few months, we have found it more stable than its predecessors, packed with more desirable features and, therefore, recommend the upgrade.

ABOUT THIS BOOK

Windows 98 Explained was written to help both the beginner and those moving from older versions of Windows. The material in the book is presented on the 'what you need to know first, appears first' basis, although you don't have to start at the beginning and go right through to the end. The more experienced user can start from any section, as they have been designed to be self-contained.

Windows 98 is a 32-bit operating system with a Graphical User Interface (GUI) front end, and includes built in accessories like a text editor, paint program and many other multi-media, networking and electronic communication features, most of which are examined in this book. Getting to grips with Windows 98, as described, will also reduce the learning curve when it comes to using other Windows application packages. For example, once you have installed your printers and learned how to switch between them and print from them, you should never again have any difficulty printing from any Windows program. Also, learning to manipulate text and graphics in WordPad and Paint will lay very strong foundations on which to build expertise when you need to master a fully blown word processor with strong elements of desktop publishing.

Windows 98 comes with the same version of MS-DOS as the one used with Windows 95, which is mainly included so that you can run DOS based application programs. If, however, you enjoy using the command line to enter instructions, you still can. We outline the process and cover the main changes to MS-DOS, but we have not attempted to cover the subject fully. If you don't work that way already, you certainly should not start now.

The book was written with the busy person in mind. You don't need to read many hundreds of large format pages to find out most of what there is to know about the subject, when fewer pages can get you going quite adequately! It is hoped that with the help of this book, you will be able to get the most out of your computer, when using Windows 98, in terms of efficiency and productivity, and that you will be able to do it in the shortest, most effective and enjoyable way.

ABOUT THE AUTHORS

Noel Kantaris graduated in Electrical Engineering at Bristol University and after spending three years in the Electronics Industry in London, took up a Tutorship in Physics at the University of Queensland. Research interests in Ionospheric Physics, led to the degrees of M.E. in Electronics and Ph.D. in Physics. On return to the UK, he took up a Post-Doctoral Research Fellowship in Radio Physics at the University of Leicester, and then in 1973 a lecturing position in Engineering at the Camborne School of Mines, Cornwall, (part of Exeter University), where between 1978 and 1997 he was also the CSM Computing Manager. At present he is IT Director of FFC Ltd.

Phil Oliver graduated in Mining Engineering at Camborne School of Mines in 1967 and since then has specialised in most aspects of surface mining technology, with a particular emphasis on computer related techniques. He has worked in Guyana, Canada, several Middle Eastern countries, South Africa and the United Kingdom, on such diverse projects as: the planning and management of bauxite, iron, gold and coal mines; rock excavation contracting in the UK; international mining equipment sales and technical back up and international mine consulting for a major mining house in South Africa. In 1988 he took up a lecturing position at Camborne School of Mines (part of Exeter University) in Surface Mining and Management.

TRADEMARKS

Ami Pro is a registered trademark of Lotus Development Corporation.

Arial and **Times New Roman** are registered trademarks of The Monotype Corporation.

HP and **LaserJet** are registered trademarks of Hewlett- Packard Company.

Intel and **Pentium** are registered trademarks of Intel Corporation.

Microsoft, **MS-DOS**, **Windows** and **Windows NT** are registered trademarks of Microsoft Corporation.

Norton Antivirus is registered trademark of Symantec Corporation.

Paintbrush is a registered trademark of ZSoft Corp.

PostScript is a registered trademark of Adobe Systems Incorporated.

Sound Blaster is a trademark of Creative Technology, Ltd.

TrueType is a registered trademark of Apple Corporation.

All other brand and product names are recognised as trademarks, or registered trademarks, of their respective companies.

ACKNOWLEDGEMENTS

We would like to thank the staff of both Microsoft and Text 100 in the UK, for their valuable help and the generous provision of software for the preparation of this book.

CONTENTS

1. PACKAGE OVERVIEW

Windows 98, just like its predecessor Windows 95, is a Graphical Interface which not only acts as a graphical front end to the Disc Operating System (DOS), but actually replaces it.

Both Windows 95 and Windows 98 adopt the **Start** button, shown below, which is always visible on the left of the **Taskbar** at the bottom of the screen. Clicking this button opens up a cascade of menus that allow you to run programs, open your documents, manage your folders and files, and maintain your system.

Windows 98 comes with a number of new 'accessory' programs, but retains or upgrades most of those available under Windows 95, such as the word processor 'WordPad', the graphics program 'Paint', and the text editor 'Notepad'. All these accessories, new and old, as well as the new unified 'Explorer', which helps you to view local, network, intranet and Internet data simultaneously, will be discussed in some detail. Of course, Windows 98 caters for many new technological developments, but the description of some of these is beyond the scope of this book.

One of the strengths of Windows 98 lies in its ability to manage all other programs that run on your computer, whether these programs were specifically written for the Windows environment or the DOS environment. Windows allows easy communication between such programs, as well as other computers which might be connected to a network, but to what extent depends on the type of hardware at your disposal. But why upgrade from Windows 3.x or Windows 95 to Windows 98 and not Windows NT (the other 32-bit Microsoft operating system)? The answer is fairly simple: if your are running certain 16-bit applications which will not run under Windows NT, or your hardware is not up to it, then Windows 98 is the only migration path to take.

What is New in Windows 98:

Windows 98 features a range of tools that make it easier to receive personalised information from Web content providers using push technology via active channels, such as The Financial Times, New Scientist, and the BBC, but you need to subscribe. Other improvements and support for new technology include:

- Unified interface for local, network or Internet browsing.

- Internet Explorer 4.0 together with Outlook Express e-mail client.

- Microsoft Netmeeting conferencing software.

- FAT32 file system - an enhanced version of the File Allocation Table, which controls the way data is stored on a disc drive. The new system allows drives of over 2Gb to be formatted as a single logical drive, instead of having to be partitioned to several smaller ones. The conversion to the FAT32 system can be carried out by running the 'conversion' program during installation or at some later date.

- Multiple monitor/video card support.

- Automatic driver upgrades via the Web.

- Comprehensive system information utility.

- Several new troubleshooting tools.

- Support for Digital Video Disc, MMX technology, Universal Serial Bus, IEEE1394 (Firewire), and Advanced Configuration and Power Interface standards. The latter is of particular use to laptop users by improving their power-saving facilities.

In general, this version of Windows is far more polished and professional than its predecessor. For the most part, however, Windows 98 has not changed much, which should help cut the learning curve for users upgrading from Windows 95.

Hardware Requirements

If Windows 98 is already installed on your computer, you can safely skip the rest of this chapter.

To install Windows 98 according to Microsoft, you will need an IBM-compatible computer equipped with Intel's 486-based, (or higher), processor, with 16MB of random access memory (RAM) and about 195MB of available space on your hard disc for a typical installation. However, to run today's Windows' software you will need a Pentium PC with at least 32MB (preferably 64MB) of RAM and up to 295MB of hard disc space for the Windows 98 installation, depending on your system configuration.

Although it is possible to operate Windows from the keyboard, the availability of a mouse is highly desirable. After all, pointing and double-clicking at an icon on the desktop to start a program, or pointing and clicking at the **Start** button to reveal a series of cascaded menus, is a lot easier than having to learn several different key combinations.

Before you start installing Windows, make sure you are not running any memory resident programs such as 'virus protection utilities'. If you have any entries in your **autoexec.bat** file that cause such a program to run, use the **Edit** screen editor (see Chapter 9) and disable the relevant commands by adding the REM statement in front of them, then shutdown and restart your computer in the normal way.

If you are using Norton Antivirus version 2.0 or earlier, use the **Start, Settings, Control Panel** command, double-click on the Add/Remove Programs icon, and uninstall the program (see Chapter 6). If you do not follow this suggestion, you will find that this particular program causes other trusted Windows programs to hang when running under Windows 98.

Finally, you will need a formatted disc to hand to make a Windows 98 starter disc when instructed.

Installing Windows 98

The installation routine is the best we have seen. To upgrade to Windows 98, run the **setup.exe** file from the Win98 folder to be found on your purchased CD. This can be done from within an existing Windows 3.x or a Windows 95 installation, as follows:

Upgrading to Windows 98 from Windows 3.x:

1 Insert the Windows 98 CD into your CD-ROM drive.

2 From the Program Manager **File** menu, select **Run**.

3 In the Run dialogue box, type
   d:\win98\setup.exe
   where **d:** is the drive letter for the CD-ROM drive.

4 Follow the instructions on the screen as discussed on the next page.

Upgrading to Windows 98 from Windows 95:

1 Insert the Windows 98 CD into your CD-ROM drive.

2 If your CD-ROM drive is self-loading, the **Setup** program will start automatically in which case go to **4**. If your CD-ROM drive is not self-starting, left-click the **Start** button and select **Run** from the displayed menu.

3 In the Run dialogue box, type
   d:\win98\setup.exe
   where **d:** is the drive letter for the CD-ROM drive.

4 Follow the instructions on the screen as discussed on the next page.

The Installation Process:

Having started the installation process, as described on the previous page, the following screen will appear on your monitor.

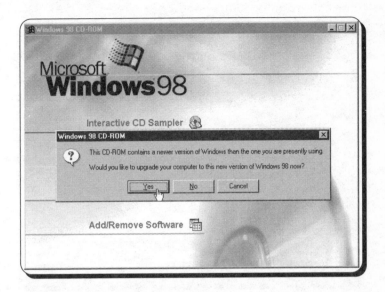

Pressing the **Yes** button displays the 'Welcome to Windows 98 Setup' screen which informs you that the process will take between 30 to 60 minutes. Upgrading our 233MHz Pentium took a good 60 minutes!

Next, the Setup program examines your system and collects information about your computer, and then prepares the Windows 98 Setup Wizard (Microsoft's way of semi-automating procedures) which will guide you through the rest of the process. The first thing that this Setup Wizard does is to display the License Agreement to which you must agree, if the installation is to proceed. Then, you are asked to type in the 'Product Key' which is made up of 5 sets of 5 letters and numbers each, to be found on the back of the CD container.

5

Next, Setup displays a screen to inform you that it is initialising your system registry database, and another while it is verifying that your computer has enough disc space to install Windows 98. If all is well, the following screen is displayed.

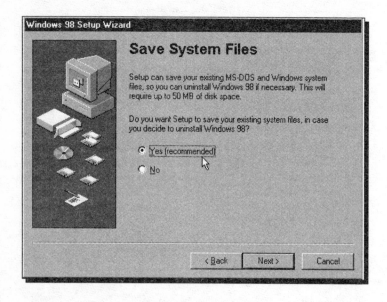

We strongly suggest that you opt to save your existing system files. This will take up to 50MB of disc space,

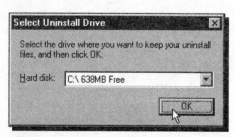

but the program allows you to choose the drive in which to save these files, as shown here. You are even given the amount of free space available in each drive. Pressing the **OK** button, saves the system files on the selected drive.

Next, Windows asks you to establish your location so that you can be supplied with news and information from the Web, as described on the screen below.

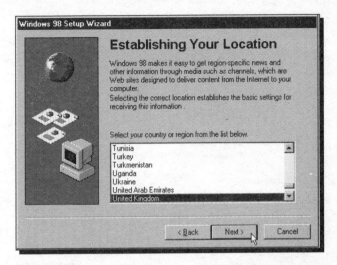

Then, Setup prepares to create a Startup disc which you will need to use to start up your system should anything go wrong.

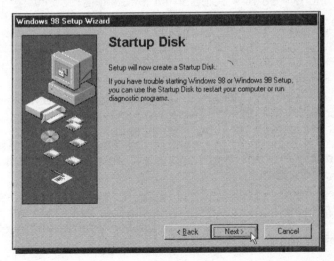

Finally, Setup restarts your computer, examines your installed hardware and software, and eventually displays the following screen.

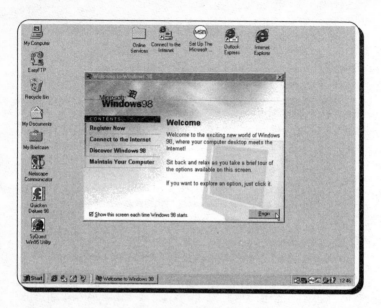

Windows 98 has detected all the installed software on our computer, leaving their icons on the desktop as they were arranged vertically on the left of the screen under our previous version of Windows. Obviously, your screen will look different, depending on the configuration of your computer.

In addition, Windows 98 has added several new icons on the desktop (we have moved these to the top of the screen for easy identification), and also a new set of buttons to the right of the **Start** button. These additional icons and buttons will be discussed in the next chapter.

In the middle of the screen, the Windows 98 Welcome screen is displayed with four self-explanatory topics. We leave it to you to browse your way through these items.

2. STARTING WINDOWS 98

Once Windows 98 has been installed successfully, switching on your PC automatically loads the operating system, and the Welcome screen is displayed, as shown in the previous chapter, unless you have chosen to deactivate this feature.

The Windows Desktop

Below we show the Windows 98 working screen, called the 'Desktop', with five items on the left of it identified as 'System icons', although EasyFTP is not part of the Windows 98 set up. In addition, the 'My Briefcase' item has been double-clicked with the left mouse button to open the screen appearing in the middle.

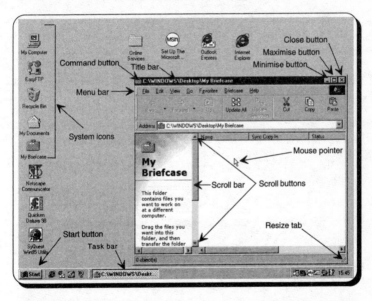

When a program is running, an icon is placed on the Taskbar. This allows you to switch between running programs by simply left-clicking them on the Taskbar.

9

Parts of a Window:

It is worth spending some time looking at the various parts that make up the Windows screen - we use the word 'Windows' to refer to the whole environment, while the word 'windows' refers to application or document windows. Applications windows contain running applications, while document windows appear with applications that can open more than one document, but share the application window's menu.

Each application, and some documents you choose to work with, open and use separate windows to run in. In order to illustrate the various parts of the Windows screen, we chose to run the My Briefcase program into whose folder you normally drag files that you want to work on at a different computer. However, although every window has some common elements, not all windows use all of these elements.

An application window is easily opened by either double-clicking its icon on the Desktop, or clicking its name on one of the cascaded menus resulting from clicking the **Start** button and selecting the **Programs** option. Although multiple windows can be displayed simultaneously, only one is the active window and displays on the top of any other non-active window. Title bars of non-active windows appear with a lighter shade than that of the active one, as shown below.

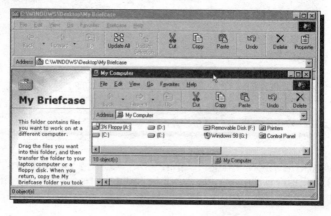

The Windows screen is subdivided into several areas which have the following functions:

Area	Function
Command button	Clicking on the program icon (see upper-left corner of the My Computer window), displays the pull-down Control menu which can be used to control the program window. It includes commands for restoring, moving, sizing, minimising, maximising, and closing the window.
Title bar	The bar at the top of a window which displays the application name and the name of the current document.
Minimise box	The button you point to and click to store an application as a symbol on the Taskbar. Clicking on such an icon will restore the window.
Maximise button	The button you point to and click to fill the screen with the active window. When that happens, the Maximise button changes to a Restore button which can be used to restore the window to its former size.

Close button	The extreme top right button that you click to close a window.
Menu bar	The bar below the Title bar which allows you to choose from several menu options. Clicking on a menu item displays the pull-down menu associated with that item. The options listed in the Menu bar depend on the specific application.
Scroll bars	The bars on the extreme right and bottom of each window that contain a scroll box. Clicking on these bars allows you to see parts of a document that might not be visible in that size window.
Scroll buttons	The arrowheads at each end of the scroll bars which you click to scroll the window contents up and down one line, or left and right one item at a time.
Resize tab	The area on a window which you drag with the mouse (hold the left mouse button depressed while moving) to resize the window.
Mouse pointer	The arrow which appears when the pointer is placed over menus, scrolling bars, buttons, and directory lists.

The Mouse Pointers

In Windows, as with all other graphical based programs, the use of a mouse makes many operations both easier and more fun to carry out.

Windows has several different mouse pointers, with the most common illustrated below, which it uses for its various functions. When the program is initially started up the first you will see is the hourglass, which turns into an upward pointing hollow arrow. Some of the other shapes, as shown below, depend on the type of work you are doing at the time.

The hourglass which displays when you are waiting while performing a function.

The arrow which appears when the pointer is placed over menus, scrolling bars, and buttons.

The I-beam which appears in normal text areas of the screen.

The large 4-headed arrow which appears after choosing the **Control, Move/Size** command(s) for moving or sizing windows.

The double arrows which appear when over the border of a window, used to drag the side and alter the size of the window.

The Help hand which appears in the help windows, and is used to access 'hypertext' type links.

Windows applications, such as word processors, spreadsheets and databases, can have additional mouse pointers which facilitate the execution of selected commands, such as highlighting text, defining areas for the appearance of charts, etc.

The Menu Bar Options

Each window's menu bar option has associated with it a pull-down sub-menu. To activate the menu of a window, either press the <Alt> key, which causes the first option of the menu (in this case **File**) to be activated (turned into a button), then use the right and left arrow keys to activate the other options in the menu, or use the mouse to point to an option. Pressing either the <Enter> key, or the left mouse button, reveals the pull-down sub-menu of the activated option.

The sub-menu of the **View** option of the My Computer window, is shown below.

Menu options can also be activated directly by pressing the <Alt> key followed by the under-lined letter of the required option. Thus pressing **Alt+V**, causes the pull-down sub-menu of **View** to be displayed. You can use the up and down arrow keys to move the highlighted bar up and down a sub-menu, or the right and left arrow keys to move along the options in the menu bar. Pressing the <Enter> key selects the highlighted option or executes the highlighted command. Pressing the <Esc> key once, closes the pull-down sub-menu, while pressing the <Esc> key for a second time, closes the menu system.

Items on the pull-down sub-menu which are marked with an arrow head to their right, as shown here, open up additional options when selected, as shown on the My Computer screen dump above.

The items on the menu bar of a specific application might be different from the ones shown here. However, almost all applications offer the following options:

File   Produces a pull-down menu of mainly file related tasks, which allow you, amongst other options, to 'open', 'delete', 'rename', 'copy' or 'move' a selected file, create a 'shortcut', or open the 'properties' of a selected item, and 'close' an open window.

Edit   Gives access to the most common editing tasks which can be applied on selected items.

View   Gives you complete control on what you see on your screen. For example, selecting the 'toolbars' and/or the 'status bar' options checks these options and allows their display (selecting them once more removes the checkmark and toggles them off). Allows you to 'arrange icons' in various ways and control whether 'large icons', 'small icons', 'lists' or 'detailed' lists are displayed.

Help   Activates the help window and displays an 'index' of help, offers help on selected topics, or opens a window and displays basic details of the system and the available resources.

Some applications display a '?' button on the right end of their title bar, as shown here. Clicking this button changes the mouse pointer from its usual inclined arrow shape to the 'What's this?' shape. Pointing to an object in the window and clicking, opens a Help topic.

For a more detailed description of each sub-menu item, either highlight it and read the text on the status bar, or use the on-line **Help** system.

Shortcut Menus

To see a shortcut menu containing the most common commands applicable to an item, point with your mouse at the item and click the right mouse button. For example, right clicking the My Computer icon reveals the following options:

In this case we have the option to **Open** My Computer which has the same effect as double-clicking its icon, **Explore** its contents, **Find** any file or document stored in it, **Create Shortcut** icons on the desktop, **Rename** the particular item, or see its **Properties**.

Right-clicking the desktop itself, displays the following shortcut menu:

From this menu you can select how to **Arrange Icons** on your desktop, or create a **New** folder or shortcut icon on the desktop, for your favourite word processor maybe.

Having activated a shortcut menu, you can close it without taking any further action by simply pressing the <Esc> key.

It might be worth your while to right-click the rest of the icons on your desktop in turn, to find out what the differences are between their shortcut menus. For example, you will find that the On Line Services and the Set Up The Microsoft Network icons have an additional option to **Delete** them, which you might want to consider, if you are not using these facilities. You will also find out that there is no option to rename the Recycle Bin.

Dialogue Boxes

Three periods after a sub-menu option or command, means that a dialogue box will open when the option or command is selected. A dialogue box is used for the insertion of additional information, such as the name of a file.

To see a dialogue box, double-click the My Computer icon, select **View** on the menu bar of the displayed window and **Folder Options** from its sub-menu. This opens the Folder Options dialogue box shown below with its View tab selected.

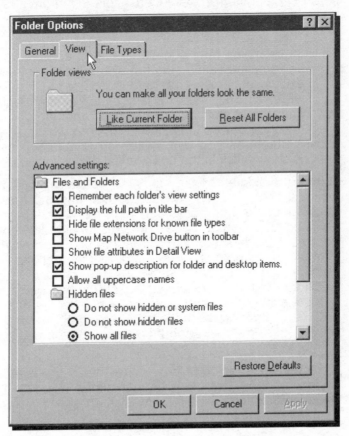

When a dialogue box opens, the <Tab> key can be used to move the dotted rectangle (known as the focus) from one field to another (Shift+<Tab> moves the focus backwards). Alternatively you can move directly to a desired field by holding the <Alt> key down and pressing the underlined letter in the field name. With the mouse, you simply point and click the left mouse button at the desired field.

Some dialogue boxes (such as the one shown on the previous page) contain List boxes which show a column of available choices. If there are more choices than can be seen in the area provided, use the scroll bars to reveal them. To select a single item from a List box, either double-click the item, or use the arrow keys to highlight the item and press <Enter>.

Dialogue boxes may contain Option buttons (sometimes called Radio buttons) with a list of mutually exclusive items. The default choice is marked with a black dot against its name, while unavailable options are dimmed. Another type of dialogue box option is the Check box which offers a list of features you can switch on or off. Selected options show a tick in the box against the option name.

Some dialogue boxes contain groups of options within a field. In such cases, you can use the arrow keys to move from one option to another. Having selected an option or typed in information in a text box, you must press a command button, such as the **OK**, **Cancel** or **Apply** button (unavailable options or command buttons are dimmed), or choose from additional options. To select the **OK** button with the mouse, simply point and click, while with the keyboard, you must first press the <Tab> key until the focus moves to the required button, and then press the <Enter> key.

To cancel a dialogue box, either press the **Cancel** button, or the <Esc> key enough times to close the dialogue box and then the menu system.

Desktop Icons and Taskbar Buttons

So far we have used the first and last of the five system icons (My Computer and My Briefcase) displayed at the top left corner of our computer's desktop, shown below. Your desktop could be arranged differently from ours and could, indeed, have different icons on it. For the sake of completeness we summarise below the function of all the 'system' icons appearing on our desktop, including that of EasyFTP which, however, is not part of the Windows 98 set up.

Double-click this to graphically browse through all your discs, folders and files.

Double-click this to reach sites on the Internet which specialise in hardware, software, and entertainment.

Double-click this to restore deleted folders and files to their original position on your hard disc.

Double-click this for quick access to the list of documents you have saved in this folder. Double-clicking a specific document in the list, opens the document and the program it was produced by, so you can carry on working with it.

Double-click this to access files you want to work on at a different computer.

The other three icons shown on our screen below the ones displayed above, are 'shortcuts' to an object. Double-clicking on such an icon opens the object itself. Later on we will discuss how to create such shortcuts.

19

Other Desktop Icons:

When installing Windows 98, the Setup program placed the following four icons on our desktop. To use any one of these requires you to have a modem connected to your computer and to a telephone line. In addition, you will be required to pay for some of the services provided.

Double-click this to list a selection of Internet Service Providers (ISPs). Double-clicking one ISP from the list invokes their Setup program.

Double-click this to start the Microsoft Network Setup program. You will be required to insert the Windows 98 CD into your CD-ROM drive.

Double-click this to start the Microsoft Outlook Express program which lets you control your e-mail. You will need to subscribe to an ISP.

Double-click this to start the Microsoft Internet Explorer which allows you to surf the Internet. You will need to subscribe to an ISP.

If you already have an Internet Service Provider, you can safely delete the first two icons from your desktop (point and left-click to highlight them, then press the <Delete> key). If, on the other hand, you intend to join an ISP, make sure to choose one that does not charge you for the actual time you are connected, through them, to the Internet, otherwise Web surfing can prove very expensive. Finally, the last two icons can also be deleted as they also appear on the Taskbar, next to the **Start** button.

Taskbar Buttons:

At the bottom of the Desktop screen is the Taskbar. It contains the **Start** button which, as we shall soon see, can be used to quickly start a program, or to find a file, and it is also the fastest way to get Help.

When you open a program, or a window, a button for it is placed on the Taskbar, as shown below.

You can left-click your mouse on this button to make this the active program, or window. So, no matter how cluttered your screen is, you can always see what windows you have open and quickly switch between them. As more buttons are placed on the Taskbar their size shrinks.

If you need to see more details on a truncated button, hold the mouse pointer over it. You can also drag the top of the bar up and have multiple rows of buttons. Try it! However, this reduces the area of the Desktop.

Next to the **Start** button, there are four buttons placed there by the Windows Setup program. These, in order of appearance, have the following functions:

1 Launch the Internet Explorer Browser.

2 Launch Outlook Express.

3 Show Desktop.

4 View Channels.

The Taskbar also shows the current time to the far right and, when installed, other icons for controlling your display (as shown above), and/or different features. Moving the mouse pointer over the clock will display the date. Double-clicking the clock, opens the Date/Time Properties box, so that you can make changes, if necessary.

Exiting Windows 98

To exit Windows, you click the START button and select the **Shut Down** option, as shown below left:

This opens the following dialogue box:

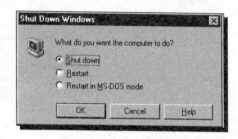

Selecting the default **Shut down** option in the dialogue box, exits all the open programs, carries out any file saves you require and then tells you when it is safe to switch off your computer. This is the only way you should end a session - never just switch off your computer without going through this procedure.

The second **Restart** option is used if you want to clear the memory settings and restart Windows 98, while the third **Restart in MS-DOS** option is used to start up your computer with the DOS prompt. This might be required by some older programs written for DOS. However, if you have problems when running DOS programs, refer to page 50 for a possible cure.

Your PC can be set up for multi-user access, with each user having their own password. If that is the case and you want to end a session, use the **Log Off** option which appears above the **Shut Down** option of the **Start** menu. This allows the current user to sign off without switching the computer off.

3. THE WINDOWS ENVIRONMENT

Windows 98 allows the display of multiple applications or multiple documents of a single application. Each of these Windows applications or documents displays on the screen in its own window, which can be full screen size or part screen size.

Manipulating Windows

To use any Windows program effectively, you will need to be able to manipulate a series of windows, to select which one is to be active, to move them, or change their size, so that you can see all the relevant parts of each one. What follows is a short discussion on how to manipulate windows.

To help with the illustration of the various points to be discussed, we will create three windows by first

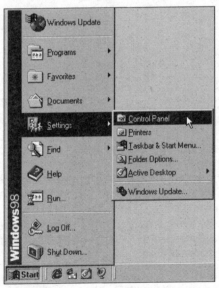

clicking the **Start** button to display the Start menu, then selecting the **Settings** option to reveal the cascade sub-menu, shown here, and clicking the **Control Panel** option. Repeat this process two more times, but click the **Printers** option on the sub-menu the second time and the **Taskbar & Start Menu** option on the third time. What you should see on your screen is shown on the next page. Don't worry about what these applications do; we will explain later.

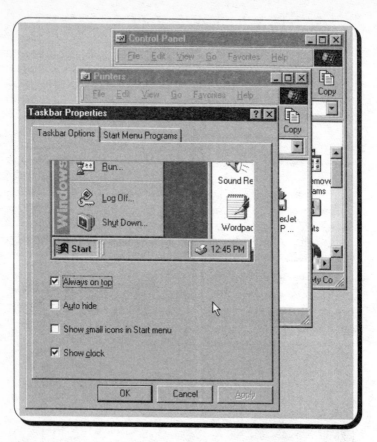

All we are concerned with at the moment is to open three windows on the screen with each window containing a different application. If the contents of the Control Panel and Printers windows do not look exactly like ours, i.e., containing large icons, again don't worry as it is not important. We simply used the command **View**, as each window was being opened, then selected the **Large Icons** option.

If you followed the order we suggested for opening these application windows, then the active window (the last one to be opened) will display on top of the others, as shown above.

Changing the Active Window:

To select the active window amongst those displayed on the screen, point to it and click the left mouse button, or, if the one you want to activate is not visible, click its icon on the Taskbar. Alternatively, hold down the <Alt> key and press the <Tab> key. This opens the

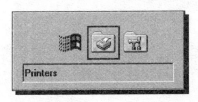

pop-up box shown here, which displays the icons of all open windows. As long as the <Alt> key is held down, the pop-up box remains visible. Pressing the <Tab> key moves the highlight through the listing and when the icon you want is selected, releasing the <Alt> key will make that the active window.

It is a good idea to practise what we are describing here. Do not be afraid if you make mistakes - the more mistakes you make the more you will learn!

Moving Windows and Dialogue Boxes:

When you have multiple windows or dialogue boxes on the screen, you might want to move a particular one to

a different part of the screen. This can be achieved with either the mouse or the keyboard, but not if the window occupies the full screen, for obvious reasons.

To move a window, or a dialogue box, with the mouse, point to the title bar and drag it (press the left button and keep it pressed while moving the mouse) until the shadow border is where you want it to be (as shown here), then release the mouse button.

To move a window with the keyboard, press <Alt+Spacebar> to open the Application Control menu, or <Alt+–> to open the Document Control menu. Then press **M** to select **Move,** which causes a four-headed arrow to appear in the title bar. Use the arrow keys to move the shadow border of the window to the required place and press <Enter>.

Sizing a Window:

You can change the size of a window with either the mouse or the keyboard. With the mouse, move the window so that the side you want to change is visible, then move the mouse pointer to the edge of the window or corner so that it changes to a two-headed arrow, then drag the two-headed arrow in the direction you want that side or corner to move.

Here we are moving the right side of the window towards the left, thus making it smaller. Continue dragging until the shadow border is the size you require, then release the mouse button.

To size a window with the keyboard, press either <Alt+Spacebar> or <Alt+–> to reveal the Application Control menu or the Document Control menu, then press **S** to select **Size** which causes the four-headed arrow to appear. Now press the arrow key that corresponds to the edge you want to move, or if a corner, press the two arrow keys (one after the other) corresponding to the particular corner, which causes the pointer to change to a two-headed arrow. Press an appropriate arrow key in the direction you want that side or corner to move and continue to do so until the shadow border is the size you require, then press <Enter> to fix the new window size.

Minimising and Maximising Windows:

Windows can be minimised into Taskbar icons to temporarily free desktop space. This can be done either by using the mouse to click the 'Minimise' button (the negative sign in the upper-right corner of the window), or by pressing <Alt+Spacebar> or <Alt+-> to reveal the Application Control menu or the Document Control menu, and selecting **n** for **Mi_n_imise**.

In the above screen dump we show the Printers window open with the mouse pointer pointing at the minimise button and also its icon on the Taskbar.

To maximise a window so that it fills the entire screen, either click on the 'maximise' button (the rectangle in the upper-right corner of the window), or press <Alt+Spacebar> or <Alt+-> to display the Application Control menu or the Document Control menu, and select **x** for **Ma_x_imise**.

An application which has been minimised or maximised can be returned to its original size and position on the screen by either clicking on its Taskbar icon to expand it to a window, or clicking on the 'Restore' button in the upper-right corner of the maximised window, to reduce it to its former size. With the keyboard, press select **R** for **_R_estore** from the Control menu.

Closing a Window:

A document window can be closed at any time to save screen space and memory. To do this, either click the X Close button (on the upper-right corner of the window), or double-click on the Control menu button (the icon in the upper-left corner of the window title bar). With the keyboard, press <Alt+–> and select **C** for **Close** from the window Control menu.

If you try to close a window of an application document, such as that of a word processor, in which you have made changes since the last time you saved it, you will get a warning in the form of a dialogue box asking confirmation prior to closing it. This safeguards against loss of information.

Windows Display Arrangement:

In Windows and most Windows application programs,

you can display multiple windows in both tiled and cascaded (overlapping) forms - the choice being a matter of balance between personal preference and the type of work you are doing at the time. If you want to organise these automatically, right-click on an empty part of the Taskbar which opens the menu shown here.

28

Below, we show two forms of windows display; the **Cascade Windows** option and the **Tile Windows Vertically** option.

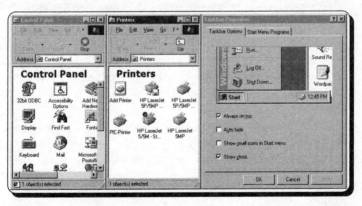

As you will have discovered by now, the size of the **Taskbar & Menu** window cannot be changed, hence you might have to alter the size of the other two to get exactly what is displayed above.

The Windows Control Panel

The Control Panel provides a quick and easy way to change the hardware and software settings of your system.

To access the Control Panel, click the **Start** button, then select **Settings** followed by **Control Panel**. Another way is to double-click the Control Panel icon in the My Computer window. Either way opens the Control Panel window shown below from which the various Control Panel options can be accessed.

Double-clicking at the Control Panel icons allows you to add new hardware, add or remove programs, change the date and time, change the display type and its resolution, change the printer fonts, and change the keyboard repeat rate.

Further, you can change the settings of your mouse, install and configure your printer(s), specify regional settings, such as the formatting of numbers and dates, and look at your system's properties. If your system is connected to the outside world or supports multimedia, then you can also configure it appropriately.

All of these features control the environment in which the Windows application programs operate and you should become familiar with them.

30

Changing your Display

If your VDU (visual display unit) is capable of higher resolution than the usual 640 by 480 pixels (picture elements), you might like to increase its resolution to 800 by 600 pixels. This will allow you to see a larger number of icons on a screen when a given application is activated. To do this, follow the steps below.

- Click the **Start** button, then select **Settings** followed by **Control Panel**.

- In the Control Panel window, double-click the Display icon.

- In the Display Properties dialogue box, click the Settings tab.

The last dialogue box is shown below with the settings changed appropriately.

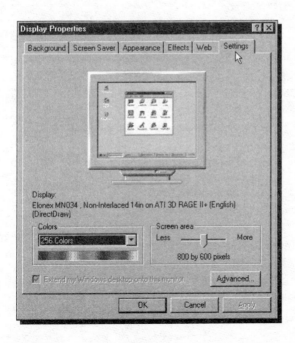

Changing the Default Printer

If you want to change the default printer, you can do so by carrying out the following steps:

- Click the **Start** button, then select **Settings** followed by **Printers**. This displays the Printers folder, shown below. Folders will be discussed in detail in the next chapter.

Here it shows that five printer drivers were installed; the first three, namely an HP LaserJet 5/5M Standard (currently the default, hence the small tick against it), an HP LaserJet 5P/5MP PostScript, and an HP LaserJet 5MP, all configured for output via the parallel printer port LPT1. The last two are configured to print to a Fax line and to a 3½" floppy disc, respectively. By the way, resting the mouse pointer on a printer icon whose label ends with three dots displays a banner with its full name in it.

- Next, double-click the icon of the printer you want to make the default printer and choose the **Printer** menu option in the displayed dialogue box. From the drop-down sub-menu select the **Set as De̲fault** option.

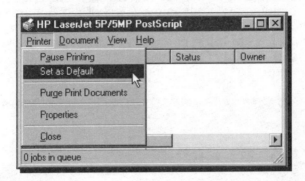

Additional Plug and Play printers are automatically detected at installation time or during the boot up process. You will be prompted for the necessary driver files if they are not already in the Windows folder. Such printer drivers are normally supplied with all new Plug and Play printers.

For other situations the Add Printer Wizard steps you through the printer installation process. You can invoke this Wizard by double-clicking the Add Printer icon in the Printers dialogue box. The choice of installing an additional printer driver could be dependent on whether such a printer was connected to your system but was not of the Plug and Play variety, or the printer was available to you at, say, your office on a shared basis. This latter option would allow the preparation of documents incorporating fonts and styles not available on the printer connected to your system, to be saved with your file and printed later on a printer which supports such enhancements. This is discussed in Chapter 6.

The Common User Interface

Although in many respects the front end of Windows 98 remains similar to that of Windows 95, the user interface has been made to resemble more closely that of the Internet Explorer 4.0 which is bundled with it. You must have noticed by now that the Control Panel, the Printers, and the My Computer windows have a toolbar with browser-style forwards and backwards arrows. The My Computer window is shown below fully extended so that all the toolbar icons are visible.

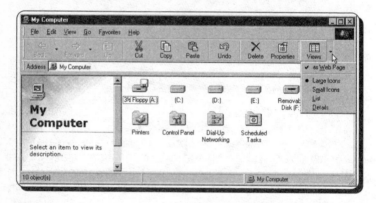

Note that to see the above display exactly as it appears, you need to click the down arrow against the Views button on the toolbar and select both the **as Web Page**, and **Large Icons** options from the drop-down menu, as shown.

Try the different display options available to you and see which one you prefer. For the display alongside we chose the **List** option. Highlighting an item, in whichever display option you operate, gives you information about that item (the C: drive in this case).

Another very useful toolbar option is the Properties button, shown here. First select a hardware item 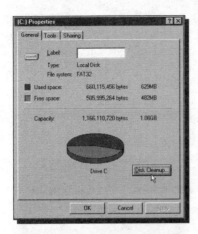 (such as a drive, a specific printer, or a document/program file), then press the button to display the selected item's Properties dialogue box.

As you can see, the Properties dialogue box for the C: drive not only contains information about it, but also gives you the option to **Label** it (give it a name), and delete unwanted files to recover precious disc space. Pressing the **Disk Cleanup** button displays the following dialogue box.

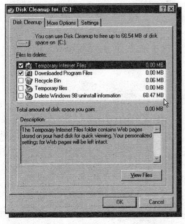

After you satisfy yourself that your system is stable and you are not likely to want to revert to the previous version of Windows, then use this dialogue box to delete all the Windows 98 uninstall files which take up quite a chunk of your hard disc.

Pressing the More Options tab on the Cleanup dialogue box displays further ways of recovering disc space by helping you to delete programs you no longer use, while pressing the Tools tab of the Properties dialogue box allows you to check your drive for errors, back up your data, and defragment your disc (more about this later).

Returning to the common user interface toolbar, apart from the View and Properties buttons, there are several others which invoke facilities that will be discussed in the next chapter. The one interesting aspect of this common user interface is, that no matter which application you are using, provided you are connected to the Internet, clicking the small globe at the top right corner of the window, shown here, will jump to a Web site without you having to load up the browser. The default Web site is that of Microsoft, as shown below.

If you are connected to the Internet, it is worth examining this facility. If not, you can always use this facility off-line and give it an address pointing to your own Home page on your hard disc, as shown below. How to design this, is another story!

Using the Help System

To obtain on-line help, click the **Start** button, then select the **Help** menu command which opens the main Help window, shown below.

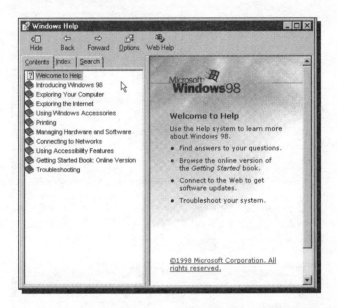

The Contents tab displays top level 'chapters', shown as book icons, which you click to open. These could contain other books or topics preceded by the question mark sign, shown here. Clicking such a question mark icon opens up a short page of text which is displayed in the right pane of the Windows Help dialogue box.

The Index and Search tabs open up interactive Help index and Search facilities. If the Index tab is clicked and you type the first few letters of a word in the input box, you are shown the available options. Selecting one and clicking the **Display** button opens its page, as shown on the next page.

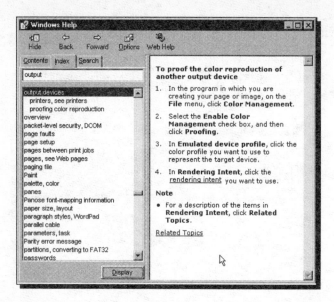

The Search tab gives you access to a very powerful individual word search facility of the Help system, as shown below.

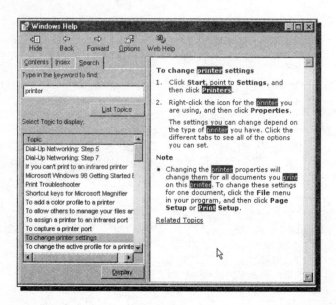

4. DISCS, FOLDERS AND FILES

Windows 98, being an operating system, controls the use of your system's disc drives and allows for the manipulation of the data stored on them. With pre-Windows 95 versions of the program you would have used the semi-graphical File Manager to look after your discs, directories and files.

With Windows 98 (and Windows 95), the way discs, folders (the old directories) and files can be handled on your PC has been changed. In the 'My Computer' facility almost everything is now done graphically, by clicking and dragging icons between windows, folders and the desktop itself. In Windows 98, as we have seen in the previous chapter, My Computer appears under the common user interface and is, therefore, capable of delivering more facilities than before.

Folders:

To see all the folders held on your computer's (C:) drive, double-click the My Computer icon on your desktop, and click the (C:) icon in the displayed window shown below.

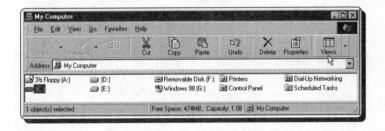

Note that for the above display, we have used the Views button on the toolbar to disable the **as Web Page** and selected the **List** option. In fact, clicking the Views button on the toolbar in succession rotates between the available display options (**Large Icons**, **Small Icons**, **List**, or **Details**).

Double-clicking the (C:) icon, displays the following:

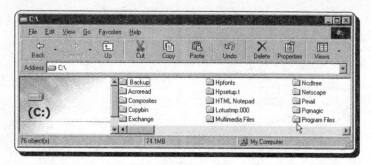

There are two points to note here: (i) the program has jumped back to the **as Web Page** view option, and (ii) the Back icon on the toolbar has been activated. Pressing this icon returns you to the previous display (the one at the bottom of the previous page), and in doing so, activates the Forward icon on the toolbar. Pressing the Forward icon displays the above screen. This simulates the way a Web browser works.

Folders are graphical devices, as shown here, similar to directories in that they can contain files, other folders and also icons. To examine this, locate the Program Files folder on your (C:) drive and double-click it to display the following:

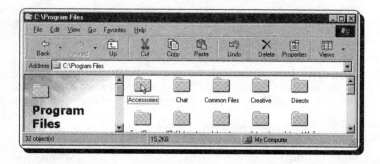

Finally double-click the Accessories folder to reveal more folders and several files.

Working with Files:

In Windows 98 you can work with files in three different ways:

- Use the My Computer utility, which Microsoft have spent much time and effort making as intuitive as possible.

- Use the Windows Explorer, a utility similar to that of My Computer, but with additional facilities.

- Use an MS-DOS Prompt window if you prefer to and are an expert with the DOS commands.

In the rest of this chapter, we discuss the first two of the above three methods of working with files.

My Computer

As we have seen, double-clicking the My Computer icon on the desktop, shown here, gives you immediate visual access to all the disc drives in your computer, as well as the Control Panel and the Printers folder. The My Computer window opens with default settings consisting of large icons, a toolbar similar to that of a Web browser, and each time you double-click an icon its contents are shown in the same window.

Icon settings are easy to change, not only from the Views button on the toolbar, but also from the **View** menu. Using the **View**, **Folder Options** command allows you to control general settings, view options, and edit the type of files you view, as shown overleaf.

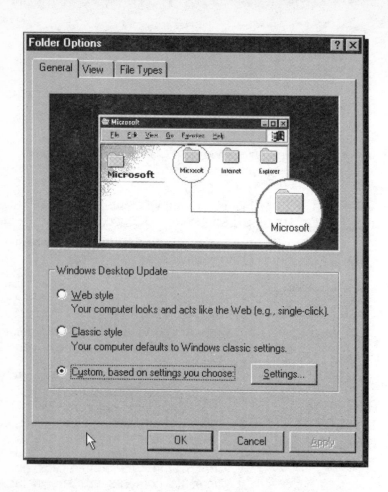

To see what program associations are valid on your system, click the File Types tab. This will open the dialogue box window shown on the next page. If you work your way down the list of **Registered file types** you can see the association details in the lower half of the box. Our example shows that an Application file has the extension .EXE. From this box you can add new associations by clicking the **New Type** button, delete them with the **Remove** button and change them with the **Edit** button.

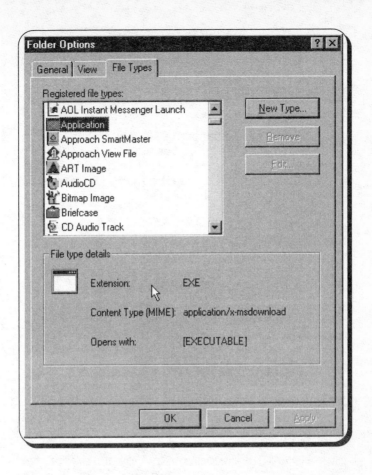

Without getting too involved at this stage, it is worth spending a few minutes just browsing through the list. It will help you to recognise the icons. These extensions are used by Windows 98 to associate files with the application that they are used with.

Any file displayed within the My Computer window, whether with its extension showing or not, can be opened by double-clicking its icon. If it is a program file, the program will run. If it is a document, it will be opened in a running version of its application program.

Creating a New Folder:

Before you start manipulating any files, create a new folder to hold copies of some existing files. It should then be safe to 'play around' with them.

To create a new folder:

- Open the Accessories folder which is located within the Program Files folder, then right-click your mouse on an empty part of the window. This opens the command menu shown to the left of the screen dump below.

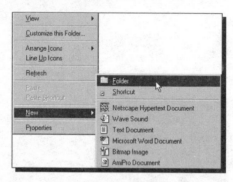

- Holding the pointer over **New** opens the cascade menu. Clicking the pointer on the **Folder** option places a new, folder on the Desktop, as shown below on the left. Its temporary name is highlighted ready for you to type its proper name.

 Type **Test Folder** into the name slot and press the <Enter> key. It's as easy as that to create and name a folder. At any time in the future you can rename it by clicking its existing name and typing in the new one. This works for files too. As you can see, with Windows 98 you can use long names (with spaces) for both your folders and your files. However, only programs written for Windows 95 and Windows 98 will recognise long file names.

44

Selecting Folders and Files:

Before selecting the folders and files you would like to copy, arrange the new Test Folder next to the other icons in the Accessories folder (viewed as large icons) as shown below.

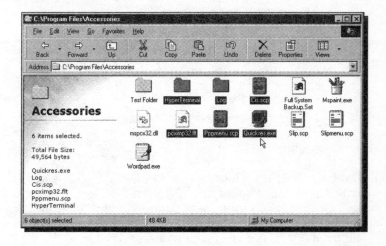

To select several objects, or icons, you have three options.

- If they form a rectangle, as above, left click one corner, then with the <Shift> key depressed, click the opposite corner.

- To select random objects hold the <Ctrl> key down and left click them, one by one.

- To select all the files and folders in a window use the **Edit**, **Select All** menu command, or the keyboard shortcut <Ctrl+A>.

To cancel a selection, you just click the pointer somewhere else in the window.

Copying Folders and Files:

As usual there are several ways to copy selected folders or icons from one window into a selected folder.

- **Using the menu:** Select the objects you want to copy, then use the **Edit**, **Copy** command from the menu bar. Double-click the folder into which you want to insert a copy of the selected objects, and use the **Edit**, **Paste** command.

- **Using the keyboard:** Select the objects to copy and press the <Ctrl+C> keyboard shortcut. Double-click the destination folder and press <Ctrl+V> to paste the objects there.

- **Using the mouse:** Press and hold down the <Ctrl> key, then drag the selected objects to the destination folder.

If the destination folder is in a different drive or a folder which is not displayed in the current window, then you will have to arrange to view each selected drive and/or folder in a different window. There are two ways of achieving this: the long way or the short way.

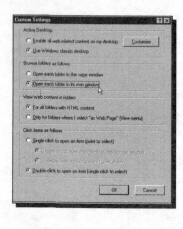

1. From the My Computer menu bar, use the **View**, **Folder Options** command to display the Folder Options dialogue box. Click the General tab, and press the **Settings** button to display the dialogue box shown here. Click the **Open each folder in its own window** option, and press the **OK** button followed by the **Close** button.

2. Double-click the My Computer icon twice.

46

In either case, you can now arrange for the source objects and the destination drive/folder to appear in separate windows, as shown below.

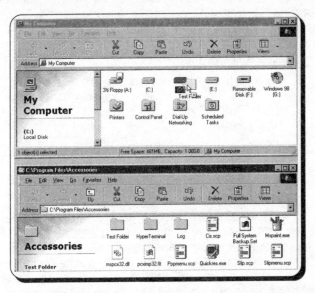

Dragging can be a little confusing until you get used to Windows 98. To drag-copy objects to a folder or window of *another disc drive*, you don't have to hold down the <Ctrl> key. This is the same action as drag-moving objects between folders of the *same* drive. Until you get used to this, take special care, or you will end up moving objects instead of copying them.

One easy way of telling what action a drag operation will result in, is to look for a + sign on the drag pointer. This indicates that a copy will take place, as shown above, where the Test folder is about to be copied to the D: drive. Perhaps a safer way of copying objects with the mouse is to drag them with the *right* mouse button depressed. When you have moved the pointer to the destination, releasing the mouse button produces a menu which gives you a choice of operations. Moving the pointer to the **Copy Here** option and clicking, will complete the operation.

Moving Folders and Files:

When you **copy** a folder or file to somewhere else, the original version of the folder or file is not altered or removed, but when you **move** a folder or file to a new location, the original is actually deleted. As with the copy operation there are several ways to move selected folders or files.

- *Using the menu:* Choose the **Edit**, **Cut** command from the source window, then use the **Edit**, **Paste** command from the destination window menu bar.

- *Using the keyboard:* Select the folders or files to move and press the <Ctrl+X> keyboard shortcut. Then select the destination window and press <Ctrl+V> to paste the folders or files there.

- *Using the mouse:* Drag the selected folders or files from one window to another, with the left mouse button depressed. This will move files between windows, or folders, **of the same drive**. But don't forget that this same operation will **copy** folders or files between different drives.

As with copying, dragging folders or files with the right mouse button depressed but selecting the **Move Here** option from the menu produced, is maybe the safest way to carry out a folder or file moving operation.

Renaming Folders and Files:

Before you rename folders or files, copy a folder into your Test Folder. Anything done to it in the Test Folder should not have any effect on the rest of your system.

- *To rename a folder or file:* First click on the folder or file icon to select it and then click the existing name below the icon. This will place a rectangle around the name and put you into edit mode. Next, type in the new name and click somewhere else, or press <Enter>, to finish the procedure. Try renaming the Test Folder to Practice Folder.

File Properties:

If you want to know more about a particular file, first select it, then either

- Click the Properties button on the My Computer toolbar, as shown below, or

- Right-click the filename and select **Properties** from the drop-down menu.

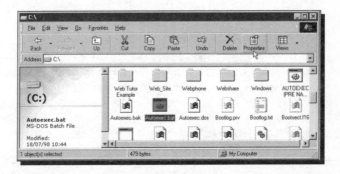

In either case, the following information is displayed:

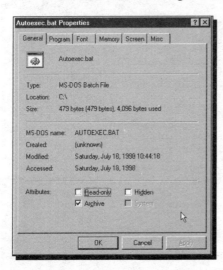

Here, the full properties of the file are listed, including its name, type, location, size, the date when it was created, last modified and last accessed. You can also change the file's attributes, by making it, say, read only, to prevent accidental changes to its contents.

49

Creating Shortcuts:

With Windows 98, just as with Windows 95, you can put a shortcut to any program, document, or printer on your desktop or in any folder. Shortcuts are quick ways to get to the items you use often; they save you having to dig deep into your system files to access them.

One program we seem to use a lot to process our system text files is the Notepad (we will discuss its use later), so we will step through the process of placing a shortcut to it onto the desktop.

You must first find the actual program. An easy way is to use the **Start, Find, Files or Folders** command and look in the (C:) drive (or whichever drive Windows is installed on). Soon enough the Notepad.exe file is found, and you can drag it onto the desktop, as shown below. This places the new shortcut icon on the desktop. Note that it has a right pointer arrow on it.

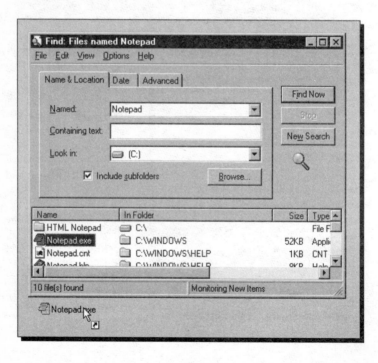

This is how you can tell that an icon is a shortcut, not the original thing. If you find the icon name a little lengthy, you can rename it, using the same procedure as described earlier for renaming files.

If your desktop does not let you place its icons where you want to, you need to change its settings. Right-click on the desktop, click the **Arrange Icons**

option on the command menu and click **Auto Arrange** to remove the tick mark alongside it, as shown here.

You should now be able to arrange your desktop icons in any way you wish, by simply dragging them around the desktop.

Sending Folders and Files:

A very useful feature of Windows 98 is the ability to quickly send files and folders to specific destinations.

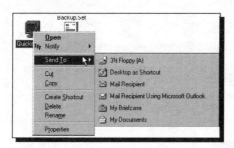

Right-clicking a selected file, or files, will open the menu shown on the left. Selecting the **Send To** option opens the list of available destinations.

Selecting the **3½ Floppy (A)** option will copy any selected files and folders to a removable disc in the (A:) drive, as shown by the very decorative animated window

that appears while the process is being carried out.

It is easy to add more locations to the Send To menu, as it is controlled by the contents of the SendTo folder, which is itself in the Windows folder. You should by now, have no trouble finding and opening this folder using the **Start, Find** command. Yours will probably only contain the same shortcut icons as ours, and you have probably worked out by now, that every shortcut held in this folder produces an option on the Send To menu.

It is useful to be able to send text files straight to the Notepad so that you can see, and maybe edit, their contents. To add Notepad to the Send To menu, simply copy the shortcut to Notepad icon from your desktop to the SendTo window, as shown below.

When you next open the menu it should have the extra item as shown here, on the right. As you can see, we have re-named the shortcut to simply 'Notepad'.

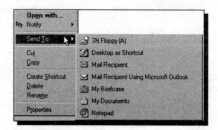

Deleting Folders and Files:

The operations described here must only be carried out on the folders or files held in the Test Folder, unless you really want to delete specific items. To experiment, copy any folder to the Test Folder first.

- To delete or remove files, first highlight them, and then either press the <Del> key on the keyboard, or press the Delete button on the toolbar, shown here, or use the **File**, **Delete** command from the window menu bar.

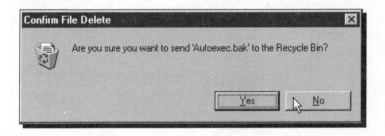

Either method opens the message box shown here which gives you the chance to abort the operation by selecting **No**.

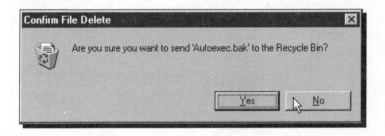

To delete folders follow the same procedure as for files. The following confirmation dialogue box will be displayed:

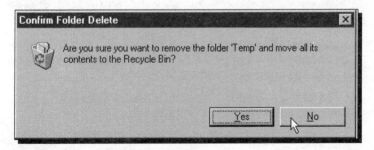

To carry on with the deletion in either case, select **Yes**.

The Recycle Bin

As you can see from the message boxes on the previous page, by default all files or folders deleted from a hard disc, are actually placed in a holding folder named the Recycle Bin.

If you open the Recycle Bin, by double-clicking its Desktop icon, you will see that it is just a special folder. It lists all the files, folders, icons and shortcuts that have been deleted since it was last emptied, as shown below.

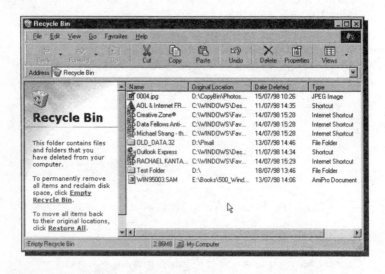

Note that Windows keeps a record of the original locations of the deleted files, so that it can restore them if necessary.

To restore files or folders, select them, and choose the **File, Restore** menu command.

To save disc space, every now and then, right-click the Recycle Bin and select the **Empty Recycle Bin** command from the displayed quick menu.

Formatting Discs

We assume, here, that your hard disc has already been formatted according to your manufacturer's instructions when setting up the system. New floppy discs must be formatted before they can be used by your computer's operating system. A floppy disc that has been formatted in one type of computer, can only be used in another computer if they are compatible and use the same operating system.

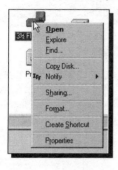

To format a floppy disc, put it into the correct disc drive, open My Computer by double-clicking its icon and right-click on the icon for the drive. In our case, this would be the (A:) drive, as shown to the left. From the displayed drop-down menu, select the **Format** option, which opens the dialogue box below. It only remains now to choose options in this box and press **Start** to carry out the formatting.

The **Capacity** drop-down list lets you select the size of disc to format. In the **Format type** section, the **Quick (erase)** option deletes the File Allocation Table of a previously formatted disc. You cannot use this on a new disc. **Full** carries out a full format, which will destroy any files on the disc (so take care). With

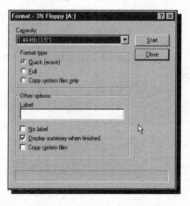

a floppy disc this option then scans the disc for bad sectors. The **Copy system files only** option places the system files onto an already formatted disc, so that it can then be used as a start-up disc.

If you want to name your disc, so that the system will recognise it by that name (in the My Computer windows, for example), enter the name in the **Label** text box. Only 11 characters will be recognised here, as with older versions of MS-DOS. If not click the **No Label** option.

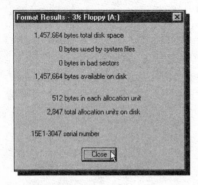

If you select **Display summary when finished** a result sheet, like the one shown here, will report on the format operation. Click the **Close** button to continue.

If you prefer, you can still use the Format command from an MS-DOS window.

Copying Discs

Copying whole floppy discs is quite straightforward with Windows 98. It is best carried out from the menu opened when you right-click the disc drive icon from within My Computer. Put the disc to copy into the drive and select **Copy Disk** from the menu.

A box, similar to that shown here, will open with your floppy disc drives listed. In our case, only one drive type shows on each side. If you have more, select the drive to **Copy from** and that to **Copy to**, but the discs must be of the same type. You can't carry out this operation between different capacity discs. When ready, click the **Start** button. You will be told when to insert the destination disc, but be warned, any files already on the disc will be lost.

Additional Features in My Computer

Microsoft has upgraded the functionality of the My Computer facility and added features previously only found in the Windows Explorer. These are mainly available in the **Details** view, and include:

- Drive sizes and their free space, including mapped network drives, are listed in My Computer's contents, as shown below.

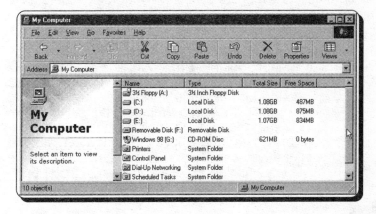

- Descriptions of the Control Panel tools are provided.

- Jobs in the print queue are listed in the Printers folder.

- Comments on other networked computers in the Network Neighbourhood can be viewed.

- Folder contents can easily be sorted by name, size, type, and modification date, simply by clicking the column title.

- Files retain their identifying icons.

In fact, as far as we can make out, there are only two differences between the new version of My Computer and the Windows Explorer, as we shall see next.

Windows Explorer

Windows Explorer is the other way of manipulating your system data. With it you can see both the hierarchy of folders on your computer (and network) and all the files and folders in each selected folder. This can be confusing to start with, but it is especially useful for very quickly copying and moving files, as we shall see. As with other system windows, the toolbar and the **View** menu let you view your folder contents in four ways, large icons, small icons, list, and detailed list.

To open Windows Explorer from the desktop, click the **Start** button, point to **Programs** and click Windows Explorer, which is probably very near the bottom of the program list, with the identifying icon shown here. When it starts, Windows Explorer shows a split window with the hierarchical 'system tree' appearing on the left, and the contents of drives and folders on the right. Your system will obviously display different contents from ours, shown below, as it is bound to be structured differently.

If you use the Views button on the toolbar to disable the **as Web Page** option, you can remove the middle pane of the above screen.

The system tree, in the left pane, lists all the resources of your computer, as well as those of a network you might be connected to. Objects which are marked with a plus sign (+), contain sub-folders. Clicking a (+) sign, opens it up to reveal the sub-folders beneath.

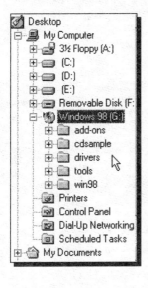

When sub-folders are displayed, the (+) sign changes to a minus sign (–), indicating that the parent folder can be collapsed. This is shown in the example on the left, where the drive (G:) (containing the Windows 98 CD-ROM) is expanded.

The right-hand, or contents, pane is automatically displayed when you select a folder from the tree. As with most Windows 98 system windows, you can change the format of the information shown in the contents pane by using the **View** commands from the menu bar, or clicking the Views button on the toolbar. All the powerful right-click and properties features described previously are supported in the Windows Explorer.

To get used to the Windows Explorer, we suggest you open it, maximise its window, set the contents format to **Details** from the **View** menu, and then slowly work your way down the system tree viewing in detail all your folders and files.

The other difference between the Windows Explorer and the My Computer facility is the addition on the latter's menu bar of the **Tools** command. Clicking this allows you to use the **Find** option, which is identical in functionality to the **Start, Find** command.

Copying and Moving Folders and Files:

Before selecting some files and/or folders to copy or move, use the Views toolbar button to disable the **as Web Page** option. Then, in the left pane, click the (+) sign alongside the (C:) drive icon to open up one level of the tree. Open the Windows folder, in the same way, and click the Command folder to open its contents in the right pane, as shown below.

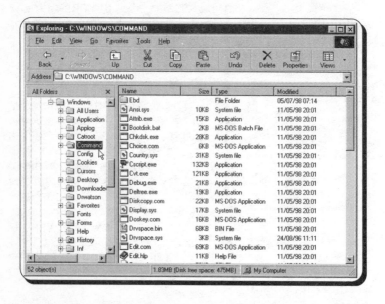

This folder actually contains all the MS-DOS command files, so make sure you don't delete any of them at this stage! If you look at the status bar it will show how many files are in the folder (ours shows 52) and how much space they take up on the disc (1.83MB).

Now, move to the left pane in the Explorer and use the scroll bar and, if necessary, the (+) icons to make sure the destination folder, (in this case a Practice folder on the (C:) drive), is visible in the tree. At this stage, do **NOT** click any of the drive or folder names, or else you will have to start again.

Next, go back to the right pane and select several files in the list, as described earlier in the chapter (for contiguous ones, by clicking the first one and with the <Shift> key depressed, clicking the last; or for non-contiguous ones, by clicking them one at a time with the <Ctrl> key continuously depressed). Once the panes are set up, right-drag the selected files from the right pane to the left and when the Practice Folder icon is highlighted, release the mouse button. This opens an option menu as shown below.

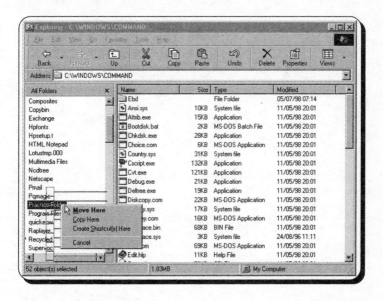

To copy the files you simply click the **Copy Here** option. If you had wanted to move them, you would obviously have chosen **Move Here**.

We think this is the easiest and, more important for a new user, the safest way of copying and moving files with the Windows Explorer, but you can also use any of the other methods described earlier in the chapter.

61

5. CONTROLLING INFORMATION

When you are using Windows 98 or one of its applications, you will invariably come across a **Readme.txt** file which contains last minute information not available in printed form in the User Guides. Vendors create such text files which can be read by either the WordPad or the Notepad Accessory. What follows, will show you how to read such files, print them, or copy them onto the Clipboard, so that you can transfer the information into another package.

Microsoft's WordPad

The updated text editor WordPad now supports new document formats (including Word 97 documents). WordPad has no pagination features, but it is a useful accessory for writing and reading simple documents or memos.

To access WordPad, click the **Start** button, and select **Programs, Accessories, WordPad**, as shown below.

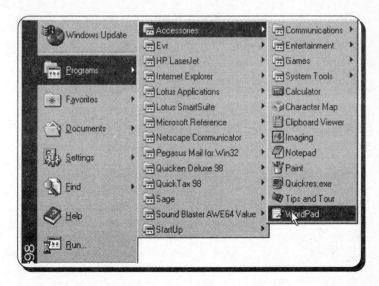

The WordPad Window:

Clicking the WordPad accessory, displays an application window similar to the one below.

The top line of the WordPad window is the 'Title' bar which contains the name of the document, and if this bar is dragged with the mouse the window can be moved around the screen. Also, just like any other window, its size can be changed by dragging any of its four sides in the required direction.

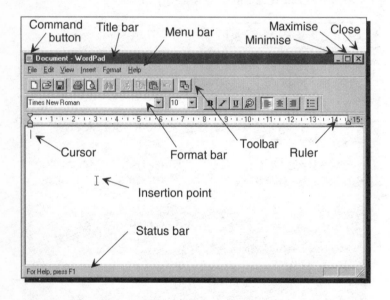

The second line of the window displays the 'Menu' bar which allows access to the following sub menus:

File   Edit   View   Insert   Format   Help

As described in Chapter 2 - 'Starting Windows 98' - the sub-menus are accessed either with your mouse, or by pressing the <Alt> key followed by the underlined letter.

The Toolbar:

As with most Windows 98 and 95 applications windows, the Toolbar contains a set of icon buttons that you click to carry out some of the more common menu functions. The actions of each icon are outlined on the screen dump below.

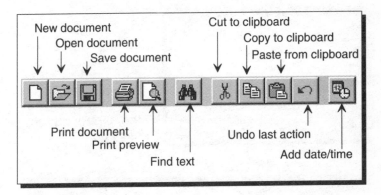

The Format Bar:

WordPad has an extra bar of icons that are used to more easily control the format of text in a document.

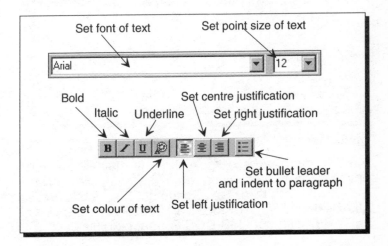

Opening a WordPad Document:

In order to illustrate this section, either type in a short letter, or if you have the Windows 98 CD, place it in the CD Drive and left-click the Open button on WordPad's toolbar, shown here, which displays the following dialogue box.

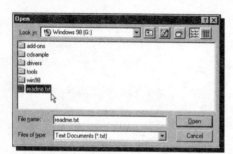

Selecting 'Text Documents (*.txt) in the **Files of type** box, reveals the **readme** file. Left-clicking this file and pressing the **Open** button, displays:

WordPad can read six types of file formats; Word for Windows (.doc) files, Windows Write (.wri) files, Rich Text Format (.rtf) files, Text Document (.txt - both ANSI and ASCII formats), Unicode Text Document (.txt) files, and Text Document - MS-DOS Format (.txt) files.

Moving Around a WordPad Document:

You can move the cursor around a document with the normal direction keys, as well as with the key combinations shown below.

To move	*Press*
Left one character	←
Right one character	→
Up one line	↑
Down one line	↓
Left one word	Ctrl+←
Right one word	Ctrl+→
To beginning of line	Home
To end of line	End
To previous paragraph	Ctrl+↑
To next paragraph	Ctrl+↓
Up one window	Page Up
Down one window	Page Down
To top of window	Ctrl+Page Up
To bottom of window	Ctrl+Page Down
To beginning of file	Ctrl+Home
To end of file	Ctrl+End

Saving to a File:

To save a document, click the Save toolbar icon, shown here, or use the **File, Save** command. A dialogue box appears on the screen, as shown below, with the cursor in the **File name** field box waiting for you to type a name. You can

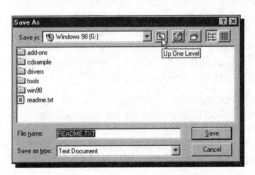

select a drive or a folder, other than the one displayed, by clicking the 'Up One Level' icon on the toolbar - the one we are pointing to.

There are five formatting choices in the **Save as type** box when you first save a WordPad document. These are: (i) Word for Windows 6 which can then be read by the latest version of Word for Windows, (ii) Rich Text Format (.rtf) which retains most of its text enhancements and can be imported into many other applications, (iii) Text Document which is a Windows ANSI file to be used if your document is a program or you intend to telecommunicate it, (iv) Text - MS-DOS format which is an unformatted ASCII file, and (v) Unicode Text Format which is another type of text file.

To save your document in the future with a different name use the **File**, **Save As** menu command.

Document Editing

For small deletions, such as letters or words, the easiest way is to use the <Delete> or <BkSp> keys. With the <Delete> key, position the cursor on the first letter you want to remove and press <Delete>; the letter is deleted and the following text moves one space to the left. With the <BkSp> key, position the cursor immediately to the right of the character to be deleted and press <BkSp>; the cursor moves one space to the left pulling the rest of the line with it and overwriting the character to be deleted. Note that the difference between the two is that with <Delete> the cursor does not move at all.

Text editing is usually carried out in the insert mode. Any characters typed will be inserted at the cursor location and the following text will be pushed to the right, and down. Pressing the <Insert> key will change to Overstrike mode, which causes entered text to overwrite any existing text at the cursor.

When larger scale editing is needed, use the **Cut**, **Copy** and **Paste** operations; the text to be altered must be 'selected' before the operation can be carried out. These functions are then available when the **Edit** sub-menu is activated, or Toolbar icons are used.

Selecting Text:

The procedure in WordPad, as in all Windows applications, is that before any operation such as formatting or editing can be carried out on text, you first select the text to be altered. Selected text is highlighted on the screen. This can be carried out in several ways:

a. **Using the keyboard**; position the cursor on the first character to be selected, hold down the <Shift> key while using the direction keys to highlight the required text, then release the <Shift> key. Navigational key combinations can also be used with the <Shift> key to highlight blocks of text.

b. **With the mouse**; click the left mouse button at the beginning of the block and drag the cursor across the block so that the desired text is highlighted, then release the mouse button. To select a word, double-click in the word, to select a larger block, place the cursor at the beginning of the block, and with the <Shift> key depressed, move the mouse pointer to the end of the desired block, and click the left mouse button.

Using the 'selection area' and a mouse; place the mouse pointer in the left margin area of the WordPad window where it changes to a right slanting arrow, and click the left mouse button once to select the current line, twice to select the current paragraph, or three times to select the whole document.

Try out all these methods and find out the one you are most comfortable with.

Copying Blocks of Text:

Once text has been selected it can be copied to another location in your present document, to another WordPad document, or to another Windows application. As with most of the editing and formatting operations there are many ways of doing this.

The first is by using the **Edit, Copy** command sequence from the menu, or clicking the Copy Toolbar icon, moving the cursor to the start of where you want the copied text, and using the **Edit, Paste** command, or clicking the Paste icon. Another method uses the quick key combinations, <Ctrl+C> to copy and <Ctrl+V> to paste.

To copy the same text again to another location in the document, move the cursor to the new location and paste it there with either of the above methods.

Drag and Drop - Maybe the easiest way to copy selected text, or an object such as a graphic, is to drag it with the left mouse button and the <Ctrl> key both depressed and to release the mouse button when the vertical line that follows the pointer is at the required destination.

As you get used to Windows 98 application packages you will be able to decide which of these methods is best for you.

Moving Blocks of Text:

Selected text can also be moved, in which case it is deleted in its original location. Use the **Edit, Cut,** command, or the <Ctrl+X> keyboard shortcut, or click the Cut icon, move the cursor to the required new location and then use the **Edit, Paste** command, <Ctrl+V>, or click the Paste icon. The moved text will be placed at the cursor location and will force any existing text to make room for it. This operation can be cancelled by simply pressing <Esc>.

Drag and Drop - Selected text, or an object such as a graphic, can be moved by dragging it with the left mouse button depressed and releasing the button when the vertical line that follows the mouse pointer is at the required destination.

Deleting Blocks of Text:

When text is deleted it is removed from the document. With WordPad any selected text can be deleted by pressing **Edit, Cut**, or by simply pressing the <Delete> key. However, using **Edit, Cut** places the text on the Windows clipboard and allows you to use the **Edit, Paste** command, while using the <Delete> key, does not.

The Undo Command:

As text is lost with the delete command you should use it with caution, but if you do make a mistake all is not lost as long as you act immediately. The **Edit, Undo** command, or Toolbar button, reverses your most recent action, so you need to use it before carrying out any further operations. The quick key for this command is <Ctrl+Z>.

Finding and Changing Text:

WordPad allows you to search for specified text, or character combinations. In the 'Find' mode it will highlight each occurrence in turn so that you can carry out some action on it. In the 'Replace' mode you specify what replacement is to be carried out.

For example, in a long memo you may decide to replace every occurrence of the word 'programme' with the word 'program'. This is very easy to do. First go to the beginning of the document, as searches operate in a forward direction, then choose the **Edit**, **Replace** command from WordPad's menu bar to open a dialogue box, like the one shown overleaf.

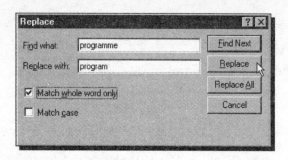

You type what you want to search for in the **Find what**
box. You can then specify whether you want to **Match
whole word only**, and whether to **Match case**, (upper
or lower case) by check-marking the appropriate
boxes. Type the replacement word in the **Replace with**
box, and then make a selection from one of the four
buttons provided. Selecting **Replace** requires you to
manually confirm each replacement, whilst selecting
Replace All will replace all occurrences of the word
automatically.

Formatting your Work

When working with text files you cannot format your
documents, but in Word for Windows, or RTF modes,
you can. Such formatting can involve the appearance
of individual characters or words, and the indentation,
addition of bullet leaders and the alignment of
paragraphs. These functions are carried out in
WordPad from the **Format** menu options or from the
Format bar.

   As an example of some of the formatting options, we
have carried out a few changes to the **Readme**
document opened earlier. First, we removed the dotted
line above and below the title. We then highlighted the
three title lines, and changed their point size to 16 and
emboldened by clicking format bar options.

The date was then added below the title by clicking the Date/Time icon on the Toolbar and choosing the date format required.

The two main paragraphs were then selected and the Bullet icon clicked on the Format bar. This indented the paragraphs and gave them bullet leaders.

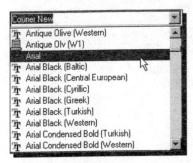 Finally, the whole document was selected and its font changed from Courier New to Arial by selecting the font type from the drop-down list shown to the left. The resulting formatted document is shown below.

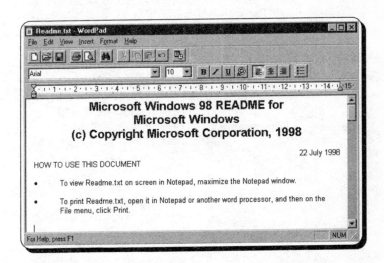

Try these features out for yourself. They are quite powerful.

The Ruler:

The Ruler, at the top of the text area of the WordPad window, lets you set and see Tab points for your text, or visually change the left and right margins, (the empty space to the left and right of the text area) of your document.

Setting your own tabs is easy by clicking within the ruler where you want to set the tab. Tabs can be moved within the ruler by dragging them with the mouse to a new position, or removed by simply dragging them off the ruler. Default tab settings do not show on the ruler, but custom tabs do.

Printing Documents

As long as your printer has been properly installed and configured, as described at the beginning of Chapter 6, you should have no problems printing your document from the WordPad application.

Setting up your Page:

Before attempting to print, make sure that WordPad is set to the same page size as the paper you plan to use. To do this, use the **File**, **Page Setup** menu command to open the dialogue box to the left. From here you can control the paper **Size** and **Source**, the size of all your **Margins** around the edge of your sheet, and the **Orientation** of the paper. The **Printer** button lets you select between different printers, and set their properties.

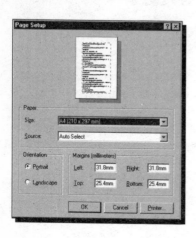

74

Print Preview:

Before actually committing yourself and printing your document to paper, it is always best to look at a Preview on the screen. This can save both your paper and printer toner or cartridge bills.

To preview the current document and settings, either click the Print Preview icon on the Toolbar, or use the **File, Print Preview** menu command to display the following screen.

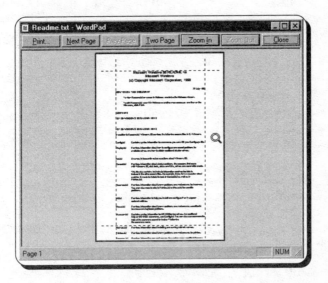

The preview screen, shown above, is the only place in WordPad that you can actually see your document's pagination, and then you have no control over it! A dreadful omission, but perhaps intentional, to make sure everyone buys Word for Windows instead!

To zoom in on the document, just click the pointer on it, or use the **Zoom In** button. If your document has several pages you can select a **Two Page** view of it. When you are happy your document is perfect, press the **Print** button.

75

Using the Clipboard

In Windows 98, you have access to the Clipboard utility which is a temporary storage location for 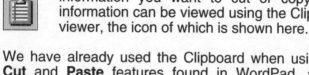 information you want to cut or copy. This information can be viewed using the Clipboard viewer, the icon of which is shown here.

We have already used the Clipboard when using the **Cut** and **Paste** features found in WordPad, and in most other Windows programs. Apart from cutting, copying and pasting operations in Windows applications, you can also use the Clipboard to copy the contents of an application's window, or to copy Windows graphics images, so that you can transfer such information to other applications. There are two ways of copying information:

• Press the <Print Screen> key to copy onto the Clipboard the contents of a whole Windows screen, even if that screen is a DOS application.

• Press the <Alt+Print Screen> key combination to copy onto the Clipboard the contents of the current open window, or dialogue box.

To illustrate these techniques follow the step-by-step instructions given below.

To Copy a Full Windows Screen:

• Close all running applications and double-click the My Computer icon on the desktop.

• Move the My Computer displayed dialogue box to the top left corner of the screen so that it does not obscure any icons on the desktop.

• Press the <Print Screen> key, then click the **Start** button and select **Programs, Accessories,** and click the Clipboard Viewer icon. The following, or something like it, will be displayed:

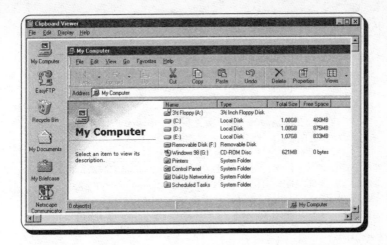

To Copy the Contents of a Current Open Window:

- Close all running applications and double-click the My Computer icon on the desktop.

- Press the <Alt+Print Screen> key, then click the **Start** button and select **Programs, Accessories,** and click the Clipboard Viewer option to display the current window only.

To copy a DOS screen:

- Close all running applications, click the **Start** button and select **Programs, Accessories,** and click the DOS Prompt option, the icon of which is shown here.

- DOS applications can run in a window or in full screen. You can switch from one to the other by pressing <Alt+Enter>. Then continue as above.

The contents of the Clipboard can be saved in a file (with the .CLP extension). The Clipboard's Menu bar supports the usual options, which are self-explanatory.

The Windows Paint Program

Paint is a 32-bit Windows application, first introduced with Windows 95 and improved with Windows 98. You can use Paint to create, view and edit, simple or complicated graphics.

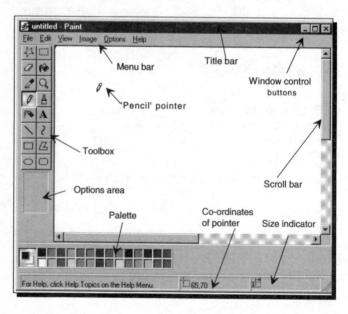

Paint is an OLE (Object Linking and Embedding) program, and allows the creation of OLE object information that can be embedded or linked into other documents, as we shall see at the end of the chapter. The Windows 98 Paint version can now read and write an increased number of file formats, namely, bitmap (.bmp) files, JPEG filter (.jpg & .jpeg) files, and gif (.gif) files.

Starting Paint:

To start Paint, use the **Start**, **Programs** command, select Accessories from the cascade menu and click the Paint entry. The following 'untitled - Paint' opening window will be displayed.

The window is divided into a 'drawing' area (the default size of which depends on your video display), surrounded by the Menu bar at the top, the Palette at the bottom, the Options box at the bottom-left corner, with the Toolbox above it.

The Paint Toolbox:

The drawing area is where you create your drawings with the help of various tools from the Toolbox. Note that the pencil tool is always selected when you start Paint, and that the function of a Toolbox icon is flagged when you move the mouse pointer over it.

To select a tool, simply point to it and click. Several of them have extra functions you can also select in the Options area. Some tools can work with either of the current foreground or background colours - dragging the tool with the left mouse button uses the foreground colour and with the right one the background colour.

More detail of the Toolbox functions is listed below.

Tool	*Function*
Free Form select	Used to cut out an irregular-shaped area of a picture, with either an opaque or transparent background, which can then be dragged to another part of the drawing, or manipulated using the **Edit** menu commands.
Rectangle select	Used to cut out a rectangular-shaped area of a picture, with either an opaque or transparent background, which can then be dragged to another part of the drawing, or manipulated using the **Edit** menu commands.

Eraser		Used to change the selected foreground colours under the eraser icon to a background colour, or automatically change every occurrence of one colour in the drawing area to another.
Colour fill		Used to fill in any closed shape or area with the current foreground or background colour.
Pick colour		Used to set the foreground or background colour to that at the pointer.
Magnifier		Used to zoom the image to different magnifications. Choose from 1x, 2x, 6x or 8x magnification in the options area.
Pencil		Used to draw free-hand lines in either the foreground or background colour.
Brush		Used to draw free-hand lines with a selection of tools and line thickness shown in the options area.
Airbrush		Used to produce one of three available circular sprays in the foreground or background colours.
Text		Used to add text of different fonts, sizes and attributes in the current foreground colour, with either an opaque or transparent background.

Line

Used to draw straight lines between two points in the current foreground or background colours and drawing width.

Curve

Used to draw curved lines in the current colours and drawing width.

Rectangle

Used to draw hollow and filled rectangles or squares (<Shift> key depressed), in the current colours and drawing width.

Polygon

Used to draw hollow and filled triangles and other polygon shapes, in the current colours and drawing width.

Ellipse

Used to draw hollow and filled ellipses or circles (<Shift> key depressed), in the current colours and drawing width.

Rounded Rectangle

Used to draw hollow and filled rectangles or squares (<Shift> key depressed), with rounded corners, in the current colours and drawing width.

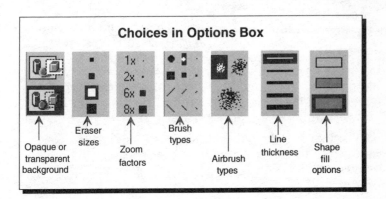

Choices in Options Box

Opaque or transparent background

Eraser sizes

Zoom factors

Brush types

Airbrush types

Line thickness

Shape fill options

81

Preparing for a Drawing

Before you start drawing, you may need to set the size

of the image you want. To do this, use the **Image**, **Attributes** menu command to open the dialogue box shown here.

The default **Width** and **Height** settings for a new image are given in **Pixels**. If you need a specific image size when it is printed to paper, you can

work in **Inches** or **Cm**. Lastly in this box, you can set whether to work in colour or in black and white. Clicking the **Default** button will make your new settings the default for any new working sessions.

Selecting Working Colours:

The current background and foreground colour settings are always shown in the two squares to the left of the

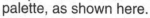
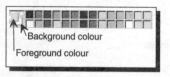

palette, as shown here.

To select a new back-ground colour, point to the colour in the Palette and click the right mouse button. If you now select

the **File**, **New** command, Paint will open a new document with the selected background colour. Alternatively you could 'flood' the existing background by selecting the Colour fill icon and right-clicking it on the background of the drawing area.

To select a different foreground colour to be used with any of the drawing tools in the Toolbox, left-click the colour in the Palette.

Entering Text in a Drawing:

If you intend to enter text within a drawing, carry out the following steps:

- Select the foreground colour for the text.
- Select the **Text** tool from the Toolbox.
- Select opaque or transparent from the options box.
- Click the pointer on the working area to open the text box, drag it to the correct size and type the text.
- Open the text toolbar with the **View**, **Text Toolbar** menu command.
- Select the font, point size or other style you want to use from the text toolbar, as shown below.

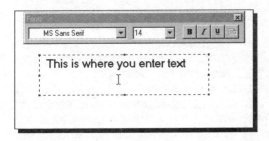

- When you are happy with the text, click outside the text box to 'fix' it in the drawing and close the toolbar.

While the text toolbar is open you can change any of its options, or use the palette, and see the entered text change straight away.

In the future, as long as the **Text Toolbar** option is ticked in the **View** menu, the toolbar will open whenever you start to enter text.

Using the Paint Tools

Most of the other tools in Paint's Toolbox are quite easy and straightforward to use. To select a tool, point to it and click the left mouse button which depresses its icon in the Toolbox. To use them, you move the pointer to a suitable position within the drawing area and drag the tool around to accomplish the required task.

With most of the Toolbox options, dragging with the left mouse button uses the active foreground colour, and with the right button the active background colour. Releasing the mouse button stops the action being performed. If you make a mistake, you can select the **Edit, Undo** command from the menu bar up to three times, to cancel the last three actions you carried out.

To complete this discussion, we need to describe how to use the 'Curve', and 'Polygon' tools, which differ slightly from the rest. For example:

To draw a curve, first click the Curve toolbar icon, choose a line thickness in the options box, left-click the pointer in the required starting position within the drawing area, then press the left mouse button to anchor the beginning of the curve and move the mouse to the required end of the eventual curve and release it. A 'flexible' line in the current foreground colour will be produced between the two points. Next, click the mouse buttons away from the line and drag it around the window, which causes the line to curve as you move the pointer. When you are happy with the produced curvature, release the mouse button.

To draw a polygon, place the Polygon pointer in the required starting point in the drawing area, left-click and drag the mouse to the required end of the first side of the polygon and release it. A line in the foreground colour is produced between the two points. Next, continue adding sides to the polygon in this way until you complete it, at which point you should double-click the mouse button.

Embedding a Graphic into WordPad:

Embedding a graphic into WordPad is similar to copying, but with the important advantage that you can actually edit an embedded object from within WordPad.

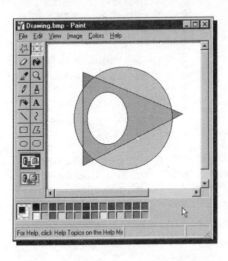

To embed a Paint image, first create it in Paint (we created the object shown to the left in order to illustrate the process), then save it as a bitmap file. Next, start WordPad, open the letter or memo you want to embed a graphic into (or just use an empty document), place the cursor where you want to embed it, and press the <Enter> key twice to make some room for it.

Now from the WordPad menu bar, use the **Edit, Insert, Object** command which displays the Insert Object dialogue box shown below. Click the **Create from File** radio button, **Browse** to locate your bitmap drawing, and press **OK** to place the selected graphic into the WordPad document, as shown on the next page.

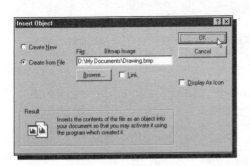

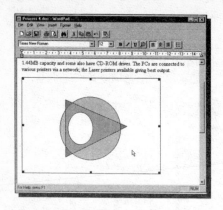

What has happened here is that the graphic has been embedded in the WordPad document. If you double-click it, the WordPad window will change to a Paint window. You can then edit the image without leaving WordPad, and clicking outside the image will bring WordPad's features back.

The **Display as Icon** option in the Insert Object dialogue box, embeds an icon in the destination document. Not much help in our example, but useful for embedding speech or movie clips in a document. Double-clicking the icon would then play the sound, or movie.

Linking a Graphic into WordPad:

Linking, the other main OLE feature, links files dynamically so that information held in one file is automatically updated when the information in the other file changes.

To link our graphic to WordPad, select the **Link** option in the Insert Object dialogue box before clicking the **OK** button. When you double-click a linked image, its file is opened into a separate Paint window. Any changes made are saved in this file as well as being reflected in the document.

These are very clever features that can save a lot of time with full Windows applications. What we have covered here should be a good grounding for the future. You must try these features for yourself, the time will be well spent.

The Notepad

Notepad is a 32-bit application, with long filename support, and has had a major change - it now supports different fonts and their modifications (bold, underline, italic). Notepad is a text editor which you can use to write short notes, or create and edit batch files. You can use Notepad to read and edit text files such as the various text (**.txt**) files supplied with Windows.

To see Notepad in operation, click its entry in the Accessories group of programs in the **Start** menu, then select the **File, Open** command and look in the Windows folder of the drive it was installed on, probably (C:). There should be several text files there. Double-clicking at the filename **Support.txt**, displays:

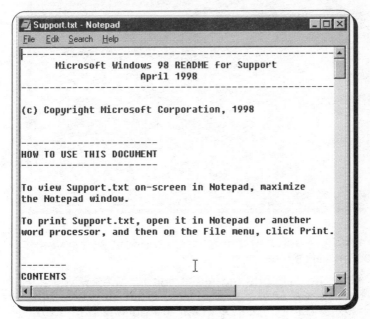

It is worth reading this file, particularly if you would like to know how to get support from Microsoft on any aspects of running Windows 98.

Notepad's Edit Features:

Although Notepad is not as powerful as WordPad, it has some interesting features, such as the ability to turn on word wrap which causes words that will not fit within its page margins to be placed on the next line automatically. You can turn word wrap on by selecting the **Edit, Word Wrap** command. Another Notepad feature is the **Select All** option from the **Edit** menu which allows you to highlight a whole document at a stroke in order to, say, copy it onto the Clipboard.

To change the font of a selected text, use the **Edit, Set Font** command to display the following screen:

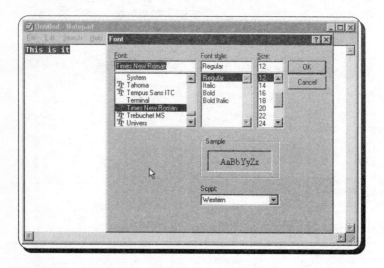

From here you can also change the font size and the font modifications.

Notepad supports the usual edit features which are useful when working with files, such as cut, copy, paste, and delete, all of which are options of the **Edit** menu. You can even use Notepad to search and find text, by selecting the **Search, Find** command. Once the text is found, pressing **F3** finds the next occurrence.

6. CONTROLLING YOUR SYSTEM

Controlling Printers

When you upgraded to Windows 98 your printers should have been installed automatically. If not you would have been stepped through the Add Printer Wizard, described later.

Nearly 1,000 different printers are supported by Windows 98 so, hopefully, you shouldn't have  too much trouble getting yours to work. The printer and printing functions are included in a single Printers folder, which you can open by double-clicking the icon, shown to the left, in the My Computer window. Our Printers folder, shown to the right, has five printers available for use, and an Add Printer icon. This folder provides an easy way of adding new printers, configuring existing ones, and managing all your print jobs.

Windows 98, just like Windows 95, supports the following printer set-up methods:

- Plug and Play printers are automatically detected at installation time, or during the boot up process. You will be prompted for the necessary driver files if they are not already in the Windows directory, these should be supplied with a new Plug-and Play printer.

- Point and Print printing enables you to quickly connect to, and use, printers shared on some other networked PCs.

89

- For other situations, the Add Printer Wizard steps you through the printer installation process, whether the new printer is connected to your PC, or on a network.

Installing an additional printer (not connected to your system, but available to you, say, at work) allows you to use the additional fonts available to this printer (we will discuss fonts shortly). Below we will step through the procedure of installing such a printer to your system.

To start installation, double-click the **Add Printer** icon in the Printers window, shown on the previous page. This opens the Add Printers Wizard, which really makes the installation procedure very easy indeed. As with all Wizards, you progress from screen to screen by clicking the **Next** button.

Having selected the desired printer on the second Add Printer Wizard screen, choose FILE: as the port you want to use with this printer on the third screen. Documents prepared with this printer selection, can then be printed to file on a 3½" floppy disc, and later printed out on the selected printer (even if it is not connected to your computer and does not itself have access to the particular application you are using).

Later you can copy that file to the selected printer from its attached PC by issuing the simple DOS command

```
COPY A:\Filename LPT1: /B
```

The /B switch in this command tells the printer to expect a binary file (with embedded printer codes).

Note that the PC which is connected to the additional printer does not even have to operate under Windows 98 for you to print your work, as the command is given at the DOS prompt. If the PC does operate under Windows 98, you will need to click the **Start** button, select **Run**, and issue the COPY command in the opened window.

Configuring your Printer:

All configuration for a printer is consolidated onto a tabbed property sheet that is accessed from its icon in the Printers folder. Right-clicking a printer icon opens

the object menu, shown on the left, which gives control of the printer's operation. If you click the **Properties** option, the sheet shown below opens and lets you control all the printer's parameters, such as the printer port (or network path), paper and

graphics options, built in fonts, and other device options specific to the printer model. All these settings are fairly self explanatory and as they depend on your printer type, we will let you work them out for your-selves.

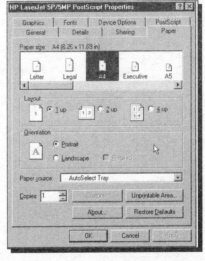

If you use one printer all, or most of the time, you should make it the default printer, by selecting **Set as Default** from its object (or right-click) menu. This saves continually having to select that printer from within your applications.

Once you have installed and configured your printers in Windows they are then available for all your application programs to use. If Windows is happy with your printer set-up, all its applications should be as well. Just make sure that the correct printer is selected by the program, which is usually one of the program's **File** menu options.

Managing Print Jobs:

If you want to find out what exactly is happening while a document or documents are being sent to your printer, double-click the printer icon, to open its window.

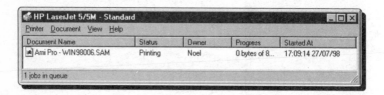

As shown above, this displays detailed information about the contents of any work actually being printed, or of print jobs that are waiting in the queue. This includes the name of the document, its status and 'owner', when it was added to the print queue, the printing progress and when printing was started.

You can control the printing operation from the **Printer** and **Document** menu options of this window, or from the right-click object menu of a particular printer's icon. Selecting **Pause Printing** will stop the operation until you make the same selection again. It is a toggle menu option. The **Purge Print Jobs** option will remove all, or selected, print jobs from the print queue.

Controlling Fonts

Windows 98 uses a Font Manager program to control the installed fonts on your system. You can use the Font Manager to install new fonts, view examples of existing fonts, and delete fonts.

To open the Font Manager, click the **Start** button then select **Settings**, and click the **Control Panel** menu option to reveal the Control Panel window, as follows:

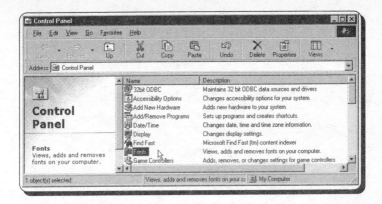

Next, double-click the Fonts icon to display the Fonts window, shown on the left below. To control what you see on the Fonts window, click **View** to display the drop-down menu, shown on the right below. We have chosen **Status Bar**, **List** and **Hide Variations**.

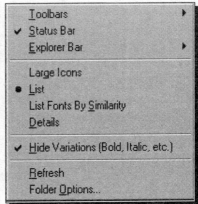

To see an example of any of the listed fonts, double-click its icon in the Fonts window. Below we show the Times New Roman (TrueType) font in four different sizes.

You might find it interesting to know, that the Symbol font contains an abundance of Greek letters, while the Wingdings Font contains special graphic objects, as shown below:

We will explain shortly how such characters can be inserted into a document.

New fonts can be installed by selecting the **File, Install New Font** menu command in the Fonts window, shown here. This opens the Add Fonts dialogue box in which you have to specify the disc, folder and file in which the font you want to install resides.

Unwanted fonts can be removed by first highlighting them in the Fonts window, then using the **File, Delete** command. A warning dialogue box is displayed.

Some Font Basics: Font sizes are measured in 'points' (a point being, approximately 1/72 of an inch), which determine the height of a character. There is another unit of character measurement called the 'pitch' which is the number of characters that can fit horizontally in one inch.

The spacing of a font is either 'fixed' (monospaced) or 'proportional'. With fixed spacing, each character takes up exactly the same space, while proportionally spaced characters take up different spacing (an 'i' or a 't' take up less space than a 'u' or a 'w'). Thus the length of proportionally spaced text can vary depending on which letters it contains. However, numerals take up the same amount of space whether they have been specified as fixed or proportional.

Windows makes available several 'TrueType' fonts which can be used by Windows applications, such as word processors. TrueType fonts are scaleable to any point size and look exactly the same on the screen as they do when printed.

Controlling Characters

A useful feature in Windows is the Character Map, shown open below. This should be found in the **P**rograms, **A**ccessories menu.

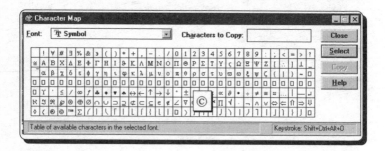

You use this facility from an application, such as a word processor, when you need a special character, such as the 'copyright' sign © above, to be included in your document.

To copy a special character, not found on your keyboard, into your document, open the Character Map, select the **F**ont, and look for that character. With high resolution monitors the characters are a little on the small side, so the one immediately under the pointer is automatically enlarged when the left mouse button is depressed, as shown above.

When you find the character you want, click the **S**elect button, which places it in the **Characters to copy** box. When you have all you want in this box, clicking the **C**opy button will copy them to the clipboard. Now, return to your application, make sure the insertion point is in the correct position and paste the characters there.

If you are observant, you may have noticed the message **Keystroke: Shift+Ctrl+Alt+O** in the bottom right hand corner of the above window. This is the keyboard code of the highlighted character.

Adding Hardware to your System

Prior to Windows 95, it was difficult to add new hardware to your PC, particularly if you did not understand how a PC works. Both Windows 95 and 98 automate this process by including a set of software standards for controlling suitably designed hardware devices.

Plug-and-Play: Windows 95 was the first PC operating system to support what is known as Plug-and-Play compatible devices. Adding such hardware devices to your system is extremely easy, as Windows takes charge and automatically controls all its settings so that it fits in with the rest of the system. So, when you buy new hardware, make sure that it is Plug-and-Play compatible.

Add New Hardware Wizard: If you are not lucky and your new hardware is not Plug-and-Play compatible all is not lost, as there is a very powerful Wizard to step you through the process of installing new hardware. Fit the new hardware before you run the Wizard, as it is just possible that Windows will recognise the change and be able to carry out the configuration itself.

If the new hardware is not recognised, start the Wizard by double-clicking the Add New Hardware icon in the Control Panel, and follow the instructions. Make sure you have no applications running, and allow the Wizard to search your system for anything new. This can take several minutes to complete, with a progress bar showing how things are going. Eventually you should be given a list of any new hardware additions that are recognised. If the search procedure dies on you, you will have to re-start your PC and try the manual option, as per manufacturer's instructions.

Add New
Hardware

Adding Software to your PC

Installing Windows applications is very easy with Windows 98. Place the first disc, or the CD-ROM, with the software on it in its drive, double-click the Add/Remove Programs icon in the Control Panel and select **Install** from the Install/Uninstall tabbed sheet, shown here. The disc drives will be searched and you will be asked to confirm what you want installed.

Add/Remove
Programs

The Uninstall option only works for programs on your system that were specially written for Windows 95 or Windows 98 and are listed at the bottom of the dialogue box. This uninstall procedure removes all trace of the selected program from your hard disc. However, with non-Windows 95 programs, you will be left with the usual application set-up files on your system.

Adding/Removing Windows Features

The Windows Setup tab of the Add/Remove Programs Properties sheet allows you to install, or remove, Windows components at any time. If you do not have a described feature on your system it may not have been installed. To install such features, open the sheet, shown to the left below, highlight the group that you think will contain them and click the **Details** button. This will list the components of the chosen group, shown to the right below. Clicking the box to the left of an item name will install the selected component, while any items with their ticks removed, will be un-installed.

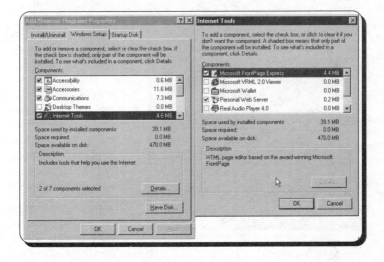

It is easy to use up too much hard disc space with Windows 98 features, so keep your eye on the **Space required** section. You will need to have the CD-ROM or original system discs available, and when you have made the selections you want, keep clicking **OK** to carry out your changes.

Checking your Regional Settings

Most Windows application programs use Windows settings to determine how they display and handle, time, date, language, numbers, and currency. It is important that you ensure your system was correctly set-up during the installation process.

Regional Settings

Use the **Start**, **Settings**, **Control Panel** command, then double-click the Regional Settings icon, shown here, to open the Properties sheet shown below.

Make sure your country setting is correct, if not, change it by clicking the down arrow to the right of the drop-down list and select the most appropriate country. You will have to restart Windows before any changes become effective.

Before leaving the Properties sheet, work your way through the tabbed pages and make sure the selections are as you want them. If, in the future, you start getting '$' signs, instead of '£' signs, or commas in numbers where you would expect periods, check your regional settings.

From this dialogue box you can also change the time and date of your computer's clock. The clock settings can also be reached by double-clicking the clock displayed at the bottom right corner of the Windows screen.

Changing the Taskbar Menus

The Taskbar menu system, as we saw in an earlier chapter, is set up originally when Windows 98 is installed, the **Start** menu being standard, but the **Programs** cascade menus being based on any previous Windows set-up you had on your computer. Once you are a little familiar with Windows, we are sure you will want to tailor these menus to your own preferences.

Adding to the Start Menu:

It is very easy to add extra programs to the top of the **Start** menu. This can be useful, as this menu opens with one click of the **Start** button which gives very rapid access to its contents.

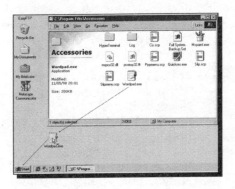

To do this, you can simply drag the program icon, or a shortcut to it, onto the **Start** button itself. For example, to add the Windows text editor WordPad to the **Start** menu, use the My Computer facility to open the Program Files Folder, then the Accessories folder, as shown above. Next, find the WordPad icon and drag it with the left mouse button depressed. When you drag a single icon like this, the drag pointer changes as you move round the screen, to indicate what will happen if you release the mouse button at that location. As shown above, the pointer is over the desktop and the small black arrow ' ' in its bottom right corner shows that a shortcut would be produced.

Over some desktop features the arrow changes to a plus sign '+' showing that the file would be copied there. Drag the icon slowly over the **Start** button. It will first seem to go under the button, then it will change to a 'No entry' sign '⊘' when over the Taskbar border, but will finally show the shortcut arrow. At that point, release the mouse button. Your **Start** menu should now have an extra option at the top, as shown here.

Within reason, you can add as many extra items to the **Start** menu as you like and they will sort themselves in alphabetical order.

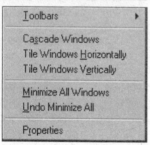

The Taskbar Properties sheet lets you both add and remove items to and from the **Start** and the **Programs** menu. To open this sheet, you select **Properties** from the Taskbar right-click menu shown here, which displays the Taskbar Properties dialogue box shown on the next page.

Clicking the **Add** button steps you, in a 'Wizard like' way, through the process of creating a shortcut to the program you want, and adding it to the required menu position. The **Remove** button lets you choose a menu item and then deletes it from the menu system.

102

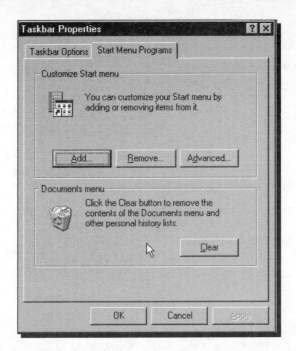

Finally, the **Advanced** button can be used to manipulate the menus in an Explorer window, as shown below. If you are happy using the Windows Explorer, this is by far the quickest way to customise your menus. This method is possible because these menus depend on the contents of the Start Menu sub-folder of the Windows folder. Menu items are stored here as shortcuts and you can add or delete them as you want.

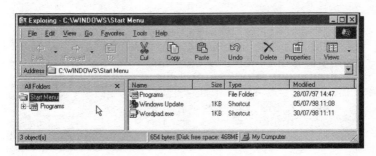

Controlling Multimedia

Windows 98 has a multitude of 'hidden' features built into it to improve the PC's multimedia performance which is simply the ability to play sound and images (both still and moving) through a computer, usually from a CD-ROM disc. These new multimedia features lead to a big improvement in both video and audio speed, quality and ease of use. As software developers bring out new programs to make use of these features, we should see a transformation in this field.

Whether all the features described in the next few pages work on your PC will depend on your system. Most of them require at least a CD-ROM player, a sound card and speakers, to be fitted and correctly set up.

Games:

We will not spend long on this topic, but many people only seem to have a PC to use it for playing games!

Our version of Windows 98 placed the four games which existed in our previous version of Windows in the Games folder, under the Accessories group. These are: Freecell - a Patience based game, Solitaire - designed to help with mouse skills, Minesweeper, and Hearts. All of these games come with quite good Help sections and we will leave it to you to explore them if you want.

Media Player:

The Media Player, with the other features we will discuss, is found from the **Start** menu by selecting Programs, Accessories and then Entertainment. The Media Player is one of the options on the cascade menu, shown to the right.

104

Next, use the **File, Open** command on the displayed
Media Player dialogue box and select a file from
the Media folder (to be found within the Windows
folder). Pressing the Play button, shown here,
starts playing the selected file.

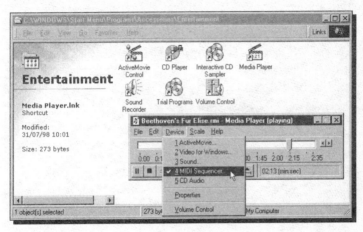

As shown above, you must first select a type of file to
play, from the **Device** menu.

To copy a multimedia file into a document is easy.
Open the file from the Media Player, open the **Edit**
menu, make your **Selection**, then specify any **Options**
you want, then finally use the **Copy Object** command.

Next, open the document you want to copy the file

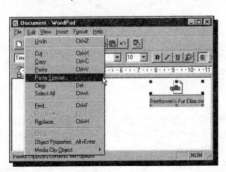

to, click the cursor
where you want it
to appear and use
the **Edit, Paste
Special** command
to paste it there,
as shown here.
Double-clicking on
the embedded
object starts play-
ing the file.

If you have the Windows 98 CD-ROM, try the **Interactive CD Sampler** option. If you don't want to lose valuable hard disc space, elect to install 'temporary files only'. Soon, files will be temporarily copied and fun pictures and music will start, ending with the screen shown below.

From this screen, you can select to see further information on 'working', 'playing', 'living', and 'learning' by left-clicking one of the options.

CD-ROM Player:

Those of you that like to have music while you work, should love the CD-ROM player packaged with Windows 98.

To run it, select CD Player from the Entertainment sub-group of the **Start** menu. This is a must for a Shortcut on the desktop, if you haven't mastered that technique yet, you should have done! The next page shows what the player looks like.

To see what all the buttons do, read the pop-up that appears when you move the pointer over them. It is well worth spending some time entering the details of your favourite music CD-ROMs with the **Disc**, **Edit Play List** option, while the particular disc is actually playing.

This not only lists the track details as they play, but lets you jump to a particular named one, to select a particular play order, or even to prevent a 'hated' track from playing at all. The Help system covers this quite well. When you next play that disc, all the details are remembered and are there for you to use.

Sound Recorder:

To record a sound, use the Sound Recorder from the Entertainment group, and while playing some music with the CD Player, press the 'Record' button pointed to below. Having recorded part of the playing music, switch off the CD Player, rewind the recorded music on the Sound Recorder and press the 'Play' button.

We have also found this accessory very useful for playing existing (**.wav**) sound files, and also for editing them. The Media sub-folder of Windows contains several such files. Use the **Effects** menu to 'play around' with the sound, and the **Edit** menu to insert and mix other sound files into the loaded one.

107

Controlling Images

Windows 98 includes an accessory by Kodak for
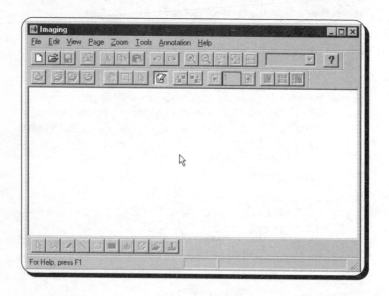controlling images. To run 'Imaging for
Windows' use the **Start, Programs,
Accessories** command, then left-click the
Imaging option, the icon of which is shown here.
After briefly showing an opening screen, the program
displays the following:

The above screen contains the usual Menu bar
command options with typical functions, such as **File**
management, ability to **Edit** your image documents,
select ways to **View** them, set your **Page** preview and
print options, and select the **Zoom**, **Tools**, and
Annotation preferences. To illustrate some of these
commands, first open the drawing we created on page
85, then spend some time investigating the various
sub-menu options available to you under each menu
command.

We now draw your attention to the top two toolbars of the Imaging screen (if you do not have an image opened, then most of these toolbar buttons are greyed out, indicating unavailability of the command or option they represent). Below, we explain briefly the function of the first toolbar buttons.

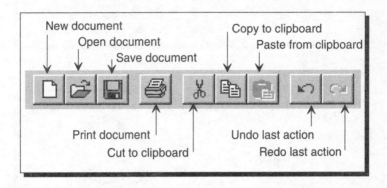

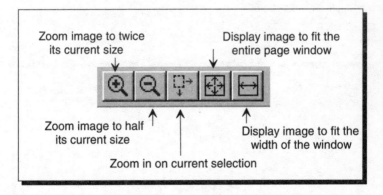

The first four buttons on the second toolbar have functions which only become active if you have a scanner attached to your system. In our case, these toolbar buttons are greyed out as we do not posses a scanner (yet!). Nevertheless, the function of these buttons is described overleaf.

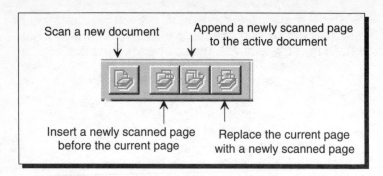

Scan a new document

Append a newly scanned page to the active document

Insert a newly scanned page before the current page

Replace the current page with a newly scanned page

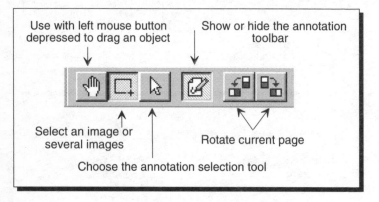

Use with left mouse button depressed to drag an object

Show or hide the annotation toolbar

Select an image or several images

Rotate current page

Choose the annotation selection tool

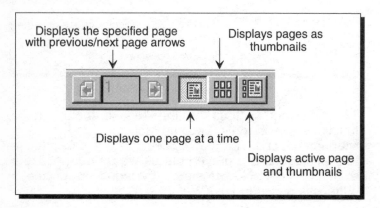

Displays the specified page with previous/next page arrows

Displays pages as thumbnails

Displays one page at a time

Displays active page and thumbnails

Finally, if the 'show/hide annotation' button is selected, then the annotation toolbar appears at the bottom of the screen, as shown on page 108. The buttons on this toolbar have the following function.

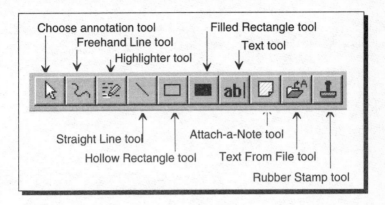

The best way of becoming familiar with the various facilities provided by Imaging, is to use a drawing you have created and play with it. If you have a scanner, then so much the better. Try it.

7. WINDOWS COMMUNICATIONS

To be able to communicate electronically with the rest of the world most users will need a modem connected, both to their PC, and to an active telephone line. This is a device that converts data so that it can be transmitted over the telephone system. Installing such a modem is quite easy with Windows 98, using the Add New Hardware Wizard described in Chapter 6.

Modem Properties

Before using your modem you must check to ensure it is correctly configured. To do this, double-click the Modems icon in the Control Panel. If Windows finds that no modem has been installed, it will step you through the process, using the relevant parts of the Add New Hardware Wizard. Otherwise it will open the Modems Properties sheet shown below.

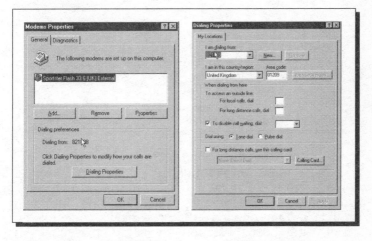

Clicking the **Properties** button will let you check the set-up of your modem. If you do not understand the settings it would be best to accept the default ones - they usually work.

Microsoft Outlook Express

To use e-mail and send faxes from your PC, you can use the Microsoft Outlook Express provided with Windows 98, or buy suitable proprietary software.

Microsoft Outlook Express has already been added to your PC by **Setup** (a shortcut icon being placed both 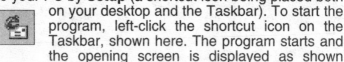 on your desktop and the Taskbar). To start the program, left-click the shortcut icon on the Taskbar, shown here. The program starts and the opening screen is displayed as shown below.

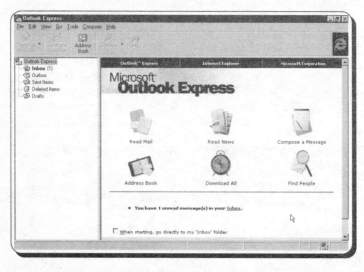

To send and receive electronic mail over a modem, you must make an arrangement with a commercial server. There are quite a few around now, and most have Internet options. Try and find one that can provide a local service in your particular area of the country, to reduce your phone bills. Once you have taken a subscription to such a service, you will be provided with all the necessary information to enter in the Internet Setup Wizard, so that you can fully exploit all the available facilities.

In the meantime you could work offline to investigate the program's capabilities. To do so, use the **File, Work Offline** command, then left-click the Read Mail icon on the opening screen. This allows you to enter the program's Inbox to read the mail sent to you by the Outlook Express team, as shown below. This mail was placed there during installation and is worth reading.

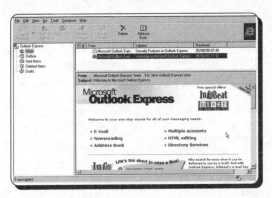

Finally, you can get a preview of the New Message screen, shown below, by left-clicking the Compose a Message icon on the opening screen.

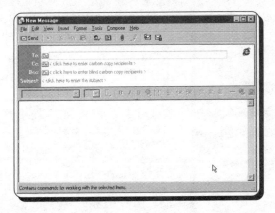

One could write several chapters on Outlook Express (which we intend to do in a separate book on e-mail), to cover every aspect of the program.

HyperTerminal

HyperTerminal also allows you to connect your computer to other computers in different locations, so that you can interchange information. You could, for example, search a library catalogue, or browse through the offerings of a bulletin board.

Before you can connect to an outside service, you need to know their communications settings. For example, you need to know the settings for 'maximum speed', 'data bits', 'stop bits', and 'parity', though most of these can be safely assumed to be the same as the default values offered by HyperTerminal. Finally, before you can make the connection, you might need your credit card and to know a password or two, as these services are not free.

Starting HyperTerminal:

To start HyperTerminal, click the **Start** button, point to Programs, Accessories, Communications.

This opens the window shown here, which is set to Large Icons. As you can see, it gives access to several communications services, such as Dial-Up Networking and Phone Dialer, both of which will be discussed shortly.

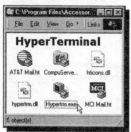

Double-clicking the Hyper-Terminal icon displays a further window which gives access to several mail services, such as CompuServe. If you want to subscribe to any of them, that is the easy way to start. Double-clicking the Hypertrm icon starts the HyperTerminal itself.

If this is the first time that you have accessed Hyper Terminal, the colourful window shown here is opened to help you make your first connection.

Every call connection in HyperTerminal can be named and saved with an icon, so that in future it is very easy to re-call the same number. After typing in a connection name, click the **OK** button which opens the next window, in which you enter the phone number of the site you want to connect to. Make sure the modem is correctly selected and press **OK** again to display the Connect window shown to the left.

To use the default modem settings, just click the **Dial** button to attempt a connection. To call the same number again in the future, use the **File**, **Open** command and double-click its name in the Open dialogue box, as shown above.

For more information about how to use HyperTerminal, click its Help menu and browse through the Contents section.

117

Specifying Communications Settings:

If you have trouble getting through, you may need to fine tune the settings. Any time a call is 'open' in the HyperTerminal window use the **File**, **Properties** menu command to change call settings, or if necessary, to **Configure** the modem so that it speaks the same 'language' as the remote system. This opens the tabbed dialogue box shown below.

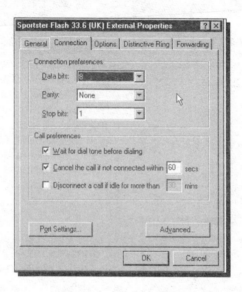

Normally, you will find that the default parameters in this are the ones you want to use. However, in case you need to change them, we list below some alternatives and their usage.

Option	*Result*
Maximum speed	Specifies the transmission, or baud, rate at which your system sends and receives data. The type of modem attached to your system determines the rate.

Data Bits	Specifies the number of data bits (binary digits) that each data packet, sent or received, contains.
Stop Bits	Specifies the time between transmitted characters.
Parity	Allows you to specify how the receiving computer verifies the accuracy of the data you are sending.
Flow Control	Allows you to specify what HyperTerminal should do if its buffer fills up during data reception. Xon/Xoff tells HyperTerminal to pause when the buffer fills, and to send a message to the remote system when ready to receive more data.

Setting Terminal Preferences:

The terminal type used by the destination site will determine the terminal type which should be used for a connection. HyperTerminal supports several common types, but in most cases the Auto detect option will sort this out automatically.

To make a manual selection, click the Settings tab of the New Connection Properties sheet, as shown overleaf on the left, with the **Emulation** list open. Select the correct terminal option and then click **Terminal Setup** to set its preferences. The set-up shown on the right above is for the VT100 selected in the main settings sheet.

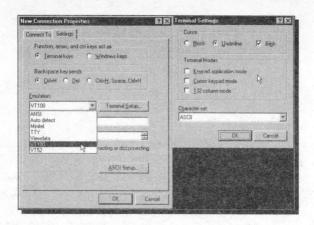

File Transfer Protocols:

Before you can send or receive files, use the Hyper-Terminal's **Transfer** command to specify the transfer protocol in either the **Send File**, or **Receive File** operation. The type of files you send or receive will be either text or binary files.

Text files: are normally prepared with a text editor or a word processor, such as WordPad or Notepad, but saved unformatted in ASCII format with only a few formatting codes such as carriage returns and linefeeds. Use the Settings tab on the New Connection Properties dialogue box and press the **ASCII Setup** button to display a sheet on which you can specify the transmission parameters for this type of file.

Binary files: are normally program files which contain characters from both the ASCII and the extended ASCII character sets.

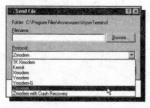

HyperTerminal supports many of the most popular protocols; which one to use depends on the receiving site. Use ZModem whenever possible as it gives the fastest transfer rates and remembers its place if your transmission is interrupted.

The Phone Dialer

If you have the facility to connect a normal telephone to your modem, you should be able to use the Phone Dialer to easily dial and log all your calls. The program can be found in the Programs, Accessories, Communications sub-group of the **Start** menu.

To make a call, simply enter the number in the text box, shown to the left, and click the **Dial** button. The down arrow will open a list of most recently used numbers. To enter numbers into the 'Speed dial' option buttons, use the **Edit**, **Speed Dial** menu command, click one of the 8 buttons, type its name and then the required number, as shown below left.

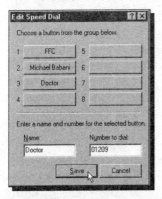

When the 'Speed dial' facility is set up, you just click one of the buttons to dial its number. To see a log of calls made or calls received, use the **Tools, Show Log** command to display the Call Log screen shown below. This gives you the name of the person you called (obscured in our example), the date, time and duration of the call.

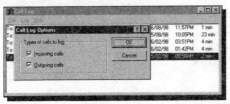

Towards the Mobile Office

Several of Windows 98's features, just as those in Windows 95, are geared to making life a little easier for those that use computers on the move.

Dial-Up Networking:

With Dial-Up Networking, you can access shared information on another computer, even if your computer is not connected to the network. To do this you must dial directly to the network server, which controls the resources of the network. If you have a computer at home, you can dial in to your office network server and connect to your work computer. Obviously, both your computer at home and the network server at work must have modems installed.

The easiest way of starting the Dial-Up Networking set-up wizard, is to double-click the My Computer icon and then double-click the Dial-Up Networking icon shown to the right. The program can also be found in the Programs, Accessories, Communications sub-group

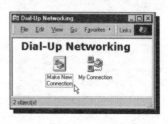

of the **Start** menu. The Wizard steps you through the process of making your first connection. After that, when you open the Dial-Up Networking window, there is an icon for every connection made, and one to help you make a new connection.

To connect to the newly make connection, double-click the My Connection icon, enter the **Password** and click the **Connect** button.

122

Using a Briefcase:

You can use the Briefcase feature to keep your copies of files updated when you work on them away from your PC. The two main uses are if you work with a mobile when away from the office, or if you transport files home in the evening on floppy discs to work on your own PC. Sooner, or later, you end up with the situation that the two sets of files are different and you don't know which one to use.

Windows 98 automatically places the My Briefcase icon on your desktop. To use Briefcase with a mobile, you connect both computers and drag the files from their folders on your main computer to the Briefcase folder icon on your mobile.

My Briefcase

When you next return to the office, after working on the files, reconnect to your main computer, open the Briefcase and click **Update All** in the **Briefcase** menu to automatically update the files on your main computer with the modified ones in your Briefcase. Sounds a little complicated, but it's not really.

To use a Briefcase with a floppy, you first move the Briefcase icon onto the floppy disc, then you drag the files you want to take home, from your main computer to the Briefcase icon on the floppy.

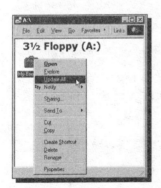

Take the floppy home and burn the midnight oil, using the files from the Briefcase. No need to copy them anywhere, but obviously make sure you save your work back to the Briefcase, before packing it in.

When back in the office, open your floppy, right-click on the Briefcase icon and select **Update All**, as shown above.

123

Now to the clever bit. The window below will open, listing any files that have been amended. In our case, there was only one file. If you are happy with the suggested course of action in this window, click the **Update** button.

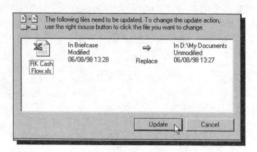

 If not, you can right-click a file name and change the action, as shown to the left. The **What's This** option gives you some help, if you need it.

NOTE: - It is essential that you close the Briefcase located on a removable disc, before you actually remove the disc from your PC. This is to ensure that the Briefcase database is updated, otherwise you will be in danger of losing data. If you are careless here, Windows tries to warn you with the message shown. If you still ignore this, you get a horrific 'blue screen DOS type' message that should wake you up!

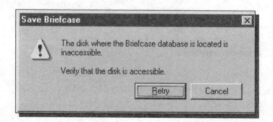

8. SYSTEM TOOLS

Windows 98, as you would expect, comes equipped with a full range of system utility programs so that you can maintain your PC's set-up as easily as possible. By default, access to all these tools is from the **Start** menu, using the Programs, Accessories, System Tools route which opens the cascade menu options shown to the right.

Backup
Character Map
Clipboard Viewer
Compression Agent
Disk Cleanup
Disk Defragmenter
Drive Converter (FAT32)
DriveSpace
Inbox Repair Tool
Maintenance Wizard
Net Watcher
Resource Meter
Scandisk
Scheduled Tasks
System Information
System Monitor
Welcome To Windows

Alternatively, you could create a shortcut directly to the folder that contains these system tools and place it on the desktop. To do this, use the Windows Explorer to locate the System Tools folder which is to be found by following the Windows, Start Menu, Programs, Accessories path. Once done, double-clicking the shortcut icon, displays all the system tools, as shown below. To see what appears here, use the **View, Large Icons** command.

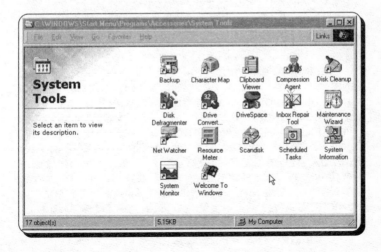

The Backup Program

Backing up both your system set-up and data files from hard disc to another storage medium, is something that everyone should do on a regular basis. Hard discs can 'crash' (though not as often these days as they used to) and your PC could be stolen, or lost in a fire, or flood. Any of these events would cause a serious data loss, unless you had backed it all up, and stored it safely.

The present 32-bit Backup utility which first appeared in Windows 95, unfortunately, is not compatible with any earlier versions. If you have any files archived with a previous Backup, or MSBackup version, make sure you keep the older DOS utilities, or you won't be able to Restore them!

If the Backup program does not appear in the System Tools folder, then use the **Start, Settings Control Panel, Add/Remove Programs** command, press the Windows Setup tab on the displayed dialogue box, locate the System Tools folder, and press the **Details** button to see what components are missing and if necessary re-install them by checking the little square against their name. This procedure holds for all the other listed programs.

Making a Back-up:

We will step through the procedure of backing up, and then restoring, a selection of files. You should then be happy to carry on by yourself. When Backup is first used, the 'Microsoft Backup' screen is displayed which has three radio buttons on its window. These determine whether to **Create a new backup job**, **Open an existing backup job**, or **Restore backed up files**, as shown on the next page. Note that there are two dialogue boxes displayed with the active one being the Backup Wizard. We will use this Wizard for the moment, but we will come back to the other dialogue box later.

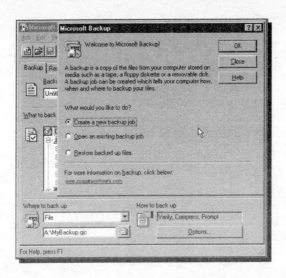

The back-up procedure can be carried out on a tape, a floppy disc, or a removable disc. In our example, below, we wanted to back up some of the files for this book, which were stored in the 456_Windows98 folder, shown in the left side of an Explorer type window.

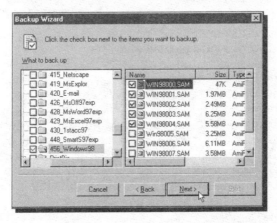

First open the tree structure by clicking the + signs, until the folder wanted is visible. To select all the files in a folder, click the small box to its left to check it.

To select, or de-select, individual files, tick in their boxes in the right hand pane and press the **Next** button. The Backup Wizard asks you to select what and where to back up, give a name to your back-up file that means something to you in the future (we called ours Win-98 Book), and **Start** the process.

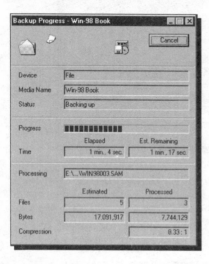

The window shown here, keeps you informed during the backing up process. In our case the 5 files of 17.091MB took 4 minutes 23 seconds to back up on two 1.44MB floppy discs, including verification (which took about half the total time). In other words the selected files, which contained lots of graphics, were very well compressed.

Now let us return to the opening screen with the two dialogue boxes by re-activating the Backup utility. To close the active window (that of the Backup Wizard), click the **Close** button to reveal the Backup utility without the interference of the Wizard, as shown on the next page. In fact, to stop the Wizard reappearing, use the **Tools, Preferences** command to open the dialogue box shown here. Next, click the **Show startup**

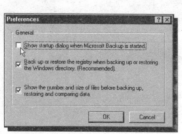

dialog when Microsoft Backup is started box to remove the tick mark, and press **OK**. The Backup and Restore Wizards can be reactivated from the **Tools** sub-menu.

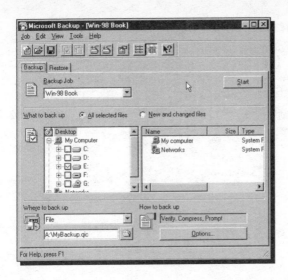

In fact, the backing up procedure is exactly the same as when using the Wizard, except that you have more flexibility. For example, have a look at the **Options** available to you when backing up. As you can see from

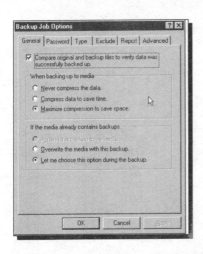

the displayed multi-tab dialogue box, shown to the left, you have many choices to make. Do spend some time looking at all the options offered, including Password protection, Type of back-up (to be discussed shortly) and whether you want to back up your Windows Registry, which we highly recommend. This last option can be reached by pressing

the Advanced tab. If you make any changes, press the **Apply** button before pressing **OK**.

Restoring your Files:

To restore files that have been previously backed up, place the first disc of the set in the disc drive, click the Restore tab of the Backup utility and the program will refresh your screen and let you select the name of the back-up set, as shown below.

Again, pressing the **Options** button reveals a multi-tab

dialogue box as shown here, which allows you to select what to do. You can, for example select to **Replace the file on my computer only if the file is older** which will save time, but also allow you to replace changed files. Again, under the Advanced tab you have the choice of replacing the Windows Registry, or not.

Types of Back-ups:

The Backup program will perform two types of back-ups, depending on the selection made on the dialogue box opened by pressing the **Options** button, with the **Type** tab pressed:

Full   Backs up all selected files, regardless of whether or not they have changed since the last back-up, and lowers the archive flags. This is the default option.

Incremental   Backs up all selected files that have changed since the last full or incremental back-up, and lowers the archive flags. This type is for the partial back-ups in your back-up cycle, if you work with different files each day. With this method it is important to save all incremental back-up sets between full back-ups.

A Back-up Strategy:

Hopefully you should by now be completely sold on the Backup program we have been using. It is only any use though if you use it systematically and with discipline. We suggest the following full and incremental back-up procedure if you generally work with different files, and create new ones, each day.

You have to keep the full back-up set with all incremental back-up sets. This is important since each incremental back-up records a different increment of changes. Also make sure the General Options tab, the **Overwrite the media with this backup** is **NOT** selected.

To use the incremental back-up procedure:

1 Perform a full back-up of all your data files.

131

2   Each day, before you switch off, perform an incremental back-up. Use the same floppy disc until it fills up, then start another disc.

3   Save all your floppy discs from the cycle until after you have performed the next full back-up.

4   Perform the next full back-up, maybe after one or two weeks, **using different discs**.

5   Perform the daily incremental back-ups as in step 2, and repeat the cycle.

It is also important to look after your back-up disc sets. Label them carefully and write the set name on all of them. Also make sure you keep each complete set together, and if your data is very important, keep the back-up sets well away from the computer, and from each other.

Disc Cleanup

You can run Disk Cleanup to help you free up space on your hard drive. Disk Cleanup searches your drive, and then lists temporary files, Internet cache files, and unnecessary program files that you can safely delete, as shown here.

As you can see, in our case, we could free 68.47MB of disc space, by simply deleting the Windows 98 uninstall information. The More Options tab allows you to remove Windows components and installed programs that you do not use any more.

ScanDisk

ScanDisk is a disc checking and repair tool designed to help check the integrity of discs and to fix any problems that are found. It is a graphical application that runs under Windows, which you should find from the **Start** menu, in the System Tools sub-group of Accessories.

As shown on the left, you can run a **Standard** scan, in which ScanDisk only checks the files on your system for errors, or a **Thorough** scan, which checks both the files and the disc surface for errors. If the **Automatically fix errors** option is checked, any errors found will be sorted out.

Defragmenting your Hard Discs

The Disk Defragmenter optimises a hard disc by rearranging the data on it to eliminate unused spaces, which speeds up access to the disc by Windows operations. As is also the case with ScanDisk, you don't need to exit a running application to run the Disk Defragmenter. Choose which drive to defragment in the Select Drive box, shown here, and you can defragment it in the background while working with another application. You can watch the progress of the operation, or display it in minimal status.

For example, having selected a drive and pressed the **OK** button, defragmenting starts and the result is

shown on a compact dialogue box, as shown here.

Pressing the **Show Details** button, opens up a very colourful screen, as shown below, which you could watch for hours!

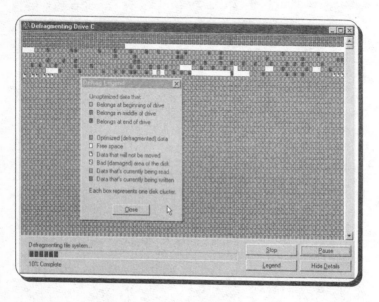

If you get fed up watching, you can always **Stop** the process quite safely, or minimise the application and let it get on with it while you work. To test what we are saying, the Defragmenter was started, the various screens captured and operated upon, then minimised to continue its job while we wrote the last two pages!

You should get in the habit of checking and optimising your hard discs regularly with these two tools.

Drive Conversion

The Drive Converter converts your drive to the FAT 32 file system (a 32-bit File Allocation Table). This is an improvement on the old FAT or FAT16 file system format, as it stores data more efficiently, therefore saving a lot of hard disc space (on our computer we gained approximately 300MB on 1,300MB of data). In addition, programs run faster and the computer requires less system resources.

However, on the down side, once you convert to FAT32 you cannot return to using the FAT16 format, unless you re-partition and reformat your converted drive! Furthermore, watch out for the following:

• Because previous versions of Windows are not compatible with FAT32, you cannot uninstall Windows 98 after conversion.

• After conversion, you can no longer use dual boot to run earlier versions of Windows or Windows NT.

• Some disc compression programs are not compatible with FAT32. If you have compressed your drive with one of these, you might not be able to convert.

• If your computer has a hibernate feature, the conversion may affect it.

• Although most programs are not affected by the conversion from a FAT16 to a FAT32, some disc utilities that depend on FAT16 will not work.

If none of the above affects you or frightens you, then you can proceed with the conversion - we actually recommend it! Therefore, as an example of what happens, we will go through the process for you, so that you can see for yourself what happens before you attempt it.

Clicking on the Drive Converter icon of the System Tools starts the program, and the following screen is displayed:

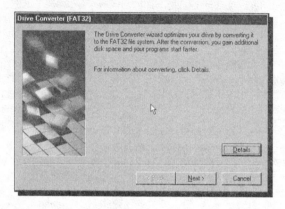

Pressing the **Next** button, causes the program to scan your system and, in our case, report the following:

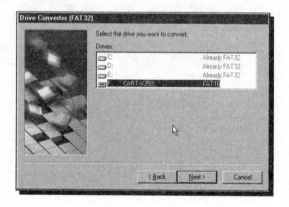

As you can see, our drives (C:), (D:), and (E:) are already converted to FAT32 , but not our removable drive which is shown above as drive (F:). To convert a drive, select it by highlighting it and press the **Next** button.

In our case, because the selected drive was a removable drive, the following warning was displayed:

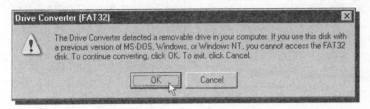

Pressing the **OK** button causes Windows to check for programs that might be incompatible with the FAT32 system, and if it does not find any, it gives you the opportunity to create a back-up of your files before conversion starts. The next displayed dialogue box informs you that 'the entire process might take a few hours'!

If you continue, the program performs a ScanDisk, then drops into a DOS screen (sic) and goes through the list below, all in less that one minute!

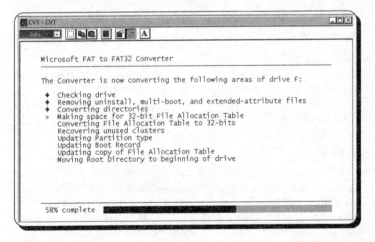

Then Windows restarts your computer and proceeds to defragment the newly converted drive which, in our case with 620MB of data, took 15 minutes to complete.

Disc Compression

Disc compression allows you to greatly increase the storage capacity of your discs with no extra hardware cost. This ability has been around for several years now, and seems to be fairly well accepted. The DriveSpace 3 utility that is included with Windows 98, is to be found within the System Tools folder.

DriveSpace 3 is compatible with the DoubleSpace compression provided with MS-DOS 6.0 and 6.2, and DriveSpace provided with MS-DOS 6.22 and previous versions of Windows. If you have drives that were compressed by using either DoubleSpace or DriveSpace, you can configure their compression by using DriveSpace 3. Because DriveSpace 3 takes advantage of improved compression, you should upgrade your DoubleSpace and DriveSpace drives to DriveSpace 3 to fully use all of its compression features. DriveSpace 3 compressed drives can be as large as 2GB.

How it Works:

DriveSpace compresses the files in a drive by a default factor of between 1.5 and 2.5 and hence lets you store much more on that drive. When you use files on the compressed drive, DriveSpace transparently uncompresses them, so that they can be accessed; and then re-compresses them when they are saved again.

This decompression and compression of files is carried on automatically in the background. This can, however, lead to a slowing down of operations, especially when moving files from one compressed drive to another. If you need to do that, we suggest you make a cup of coffee.

When DriveSpace first compresses a drive, it sets up a hidden file on an uncompressed part of the drive, which is then treated as a new logical drive. Thus for every hard drive you compress you acquire another drive letter.

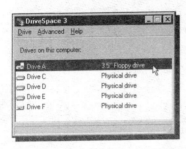

When you first open DriveSpace, a window like the one shown here, gives you the choice of compressing your floppy drive(s), as well as your hard disc drives, whether these are removable or not. To compress a drive, simply double-click its entry on the list. This opens the Compression Properties window shown below.

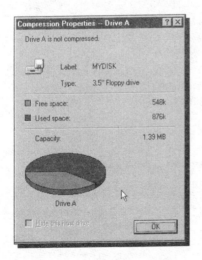

Here, we double-clicked the 3½" floppy drive. This window shows the amount of free space available on the selected drive before compression. If you have sufficient free space (to compress a 3½" floppy drive you need to have at least 512KB of free space on it), press the **OK** button, then use the **Drive, Compress** command on the DriveSpace 3 window. If you do not have enough free space on the drive you want to compress, you will be told so, and the process will be aborted, otherwise the following dialogue box opens on your screen.

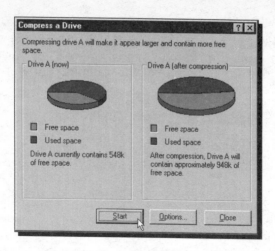

This Compress a Drive dialogue box shows the amount of free space available on the selected drive before compression and the estimated situation after compression. Clicking the **Options** button lets you fine tune the procedure, and when you are ready, clicking the **Start** button begins the process.

We do recommend that you experiment on a floppy before attempting to compress a hard disc. In any case, do read the excellent notes on compression provided within the **Help** menu option of DriveSpace 3, part of which is shown below.

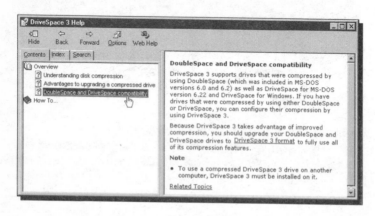

The Maintenance Wizard

The Maintenance Wizard allows you to carry out several housekeeping tasks, such as checking your hard disc for errors or defragmenting your data, at times convenient to you. Double-clicking the Maintenance Wizard icon, found in the Accessories, System Tools folder and shown here, opens the first Wizard sheet, shown below.

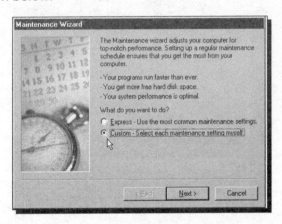

On here you specify to either 'Use the most common maintenance settings' or 'Select each maintenance setting'. We chose the latter because it gave us more flexibility, and pressed **Next**.

The next sheet of the Maintenance Wizard asks you to specify when you want these tasks to be carried out. Obviously, your computer must be switched on in order to perform such tasks, so it's up to you to choose a convenient time. Having done so, press the **Next** button to display the third Wizard sheet, shown overleaf. Our list of programs that open automatically each time Windows is started might be different from yours, but we were surprised to find some forgotten and unwanted programs.

141

Check the small square against any unwanted programs and press the **Next** button to open the Wizard sheet below.

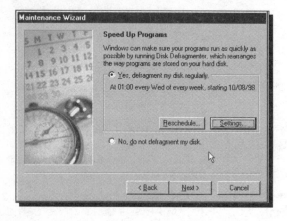

On this sheet you are asked whether you would like to defragment your hard disc regularly, and if so, you can **Reschedule** the time and frequency of the event, and also choose which drives by pressing the **Settings** button. The next Wizard sheet offers to scan your hard disc for errors, and is similar to the one above.

Next, you are asked to specify the type of files to be deleted regularly, and finally you are presented with the following display.

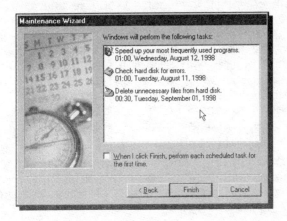

Pressing the **Finish** button, performs all the selected tasks at their chosen times, but you have the choice of having these performed immediately for the first time by checking the small square box at the bottom of the sheet.

It is a good idea to perform such tasks regularly, but make sure that (a) your computer is switched on at the selected times, and (b) you are not inconvenienced by your time selection. It is, of course assumed that your PC's clock is showing the same time as your watch, otherwise you might get some unexpected surprises!

If you have upgraded from Windows 95, you will also have the Scheduled Tasks utility in your Accessories, System Tools folder, the icon of which is shown here.

Essentially, you can perform the same tasks as those offered by the Maintenance Wizard, but you can also schedule to carry out additional tasks.

143

Windows Update

If you are connected to the Internet, you can automatically visit Microsoft's Web site and check that your computer installation has the latest versions of program drivers, program fixes, etc. The Web-based Windows Update installs a few controls and requires that you register with Microsoft first, unless you have done so previously. If you haven't, make sure you have the product key (the five sets of five letters and numbers that appear on the back of your Windows 98 CD jacket), because you will be asked to supply it.

To start the Update process, use the **Start**, **Windows Update** command. After connecting to the Internet through your service provider (ISP), you will be connected automatically to the Microsoft's Web site, as shown below.

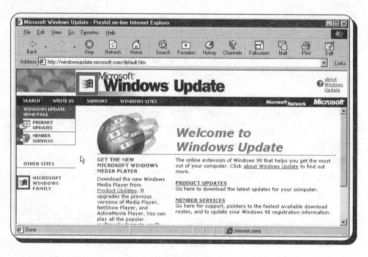

In order to be able to download program patches to your system, the program needs to have information relating to your system configuration. Such information is apparently not passed on to Microsoft. Once this is done, you can select which software to download, if any.

Next left-click the 'PRODUCT UPDATES' link, to get an appropriate list of Critical Updates for your system, together with other lists, such as Picks of the Month, etc. Be careful you don't go overboard with your selection of downloads ... think of your telephone bill!

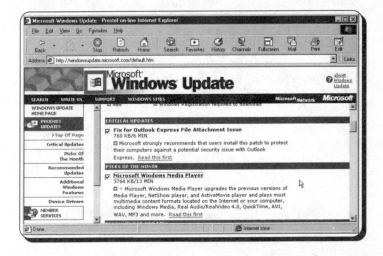

Once you have completed your selection click the DOWNLOAD button (either the one at the top of the displayed page or the one at the bottom) to see a list of your choices. Ours is shown below.

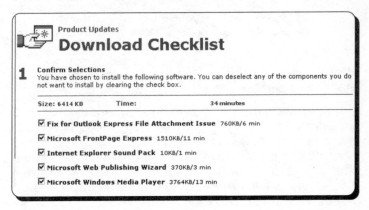

Although the total time for the download is shown as 34 minutes, this depends on a lot of factors, one of which is the speed of data transfer in your particular connection. In our case it took well over an hour to complete the job. So be careful with your initial choice.

We suggest that you download only from the list of Critical Updates. Selecting downloads from the other lists should be confined to only those you really need, and then only to one at a time. The reason for this is that should you find it takes too long to complete a given transfer, cancelling it will exit the **Setup** program and you will lose all the files already transferred before you issued the cancel command.

On successful completion of program downloads, the Windows **Setup** program installs the new patches and or programs to your system automatically and displays the following screen.

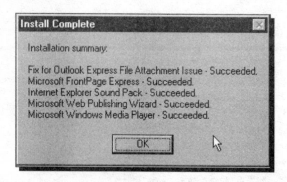

After this, you can either go back to browse Microsoft's site, or you can disconnect from the Internet.

Just to find out how intelligent the Windows Update program is, we reconnected an hour or so later, and this time we found that the program patch and the other programs we downloaded earlier were not on the offered lists. In other words, this facility works very well indeed, and gives novices the sense of being in charge of their Windows installation.

Disabling Fast Shutdown

As reported in the Preface of this book, the new rapid shutdown feature in Windows 98 has caused our system to hang several times. Since the only way we could end a session under such circumstances was to switch off the power to our PC, next time we switched on, it caused Windows to scan our hard disc for errors because we had not closed down the system properly. Below we explain how you can disable the fast shutdown feature to cure such a problem.

To disable the fast shutdown feature in Windows 98, use the **Start**, **Programs**, **Accessories**, **System Tools**

 command and click on the **System Information** entry on the cascade sub-menu, the icon of which is shown here. This opens the following dialogue box.

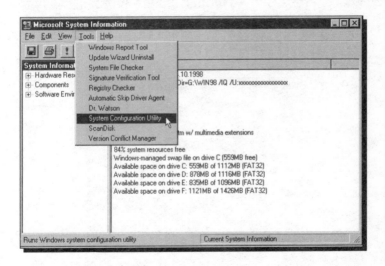

Next, use the **Tools, System Configuration Utility** command, as shown above, to open the dialogue box shown overleaf.

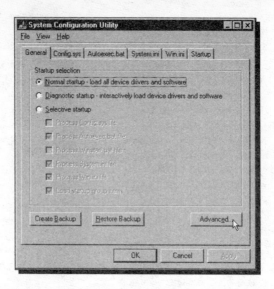

Finally, press the **Advanc<u>e</u>d** button to open the final dialogue box and check the **Disable <u>f</u>ast shutdown** entry, as shown below, and press **OK**.

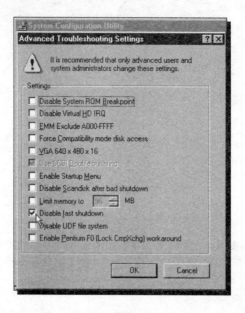

9. USING DOS PROGRAMS

If you are an experienced PC user, you may well prefer to do much of your work by entering instructions at the DOS command line, or prompt. Windows 98, just like Windows 95, still lets you do this.

For this book we have assumed that if you want to use this method of working you will already be familiar with DOS commands, switches, filters and batch files, configuration files, etc. If not, we suggest you use the methods described in earlier chapters. All the available DOS commands can be found in the COMMAND sub-directory of the WINDOWS directory. There are a few new ones, many have been made obsolete, but they all support Windows 98 32-bit features.

Before we go on with our discussion of how to run DOS programs, you might like to know that the **autoexec.bat**[1] and **config.sys**[2] files are not needed any more by Windows 98. However, if you have upgraded from previous versions of Windows, both your **autoexec.bat** and **config.sys** files are retained, with the result that it takes twice as long to start Windows as it should. The reason for this is that all the information contained in those two files (loading neccessary drivers[3] for use by your peripherals[4] into memory) are executed first, then Windows scans your system using its Plug and Play facility, discovers what peripherals are connected to your system and reloads all the drivers again!

For the benefit of inexperienced DOS users who might be reading this section, we discuss next how to remove these two configuration files from the boot-up sequence[5], and explain below some of the jargon used in the last paragraph.

---

[1] A batch file containing commands which are automatically executed on boot-up.
[2] A special file that allows the system to be configured.
[3] A set of commands loaded into memory and used to run a hardware device.
[4] Any hardware device attached to a PC.
[5] The commands executed automatically by your PC when it is first switched on.

149

Removing Configuration Files

Whether or not you use DOS programs, you no longer need your **autoexec.bat** or **config.sys** files. The easiest way to remove them from the boot-up sequence is, of course, to delete them. However, as we would like you to keep the contents of the **autoexec.bat** file for a while, we suggest that you rename it instead. To do this, use the **Start, Programs** command, and click on the MS-DOS Prompt on the cascade menu, to open the following MS-DOS window.

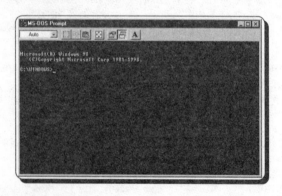

Next, type in the two lines below at the cursor position and press <Enter> at the end of each line.

```
cd\
ren autoexec.bat autoexec.old
```

The first command line changes the directory from that of \WINDOWS to the root directory where the configuration files are to be found, while the second line renames the **autoexec.bat** file to **autoexec.old**. Next, type,

```
del config.sys
```

and press <Enter> to delete this file.

When you now restart your PC, the configuration files will not be found by the booting up sequence.

The MS-DOS Window

You can action any DOS commands you like in the MS-DOS window. To view the toolbar, if it is not showing, click the MS-DOS icon in the title bar to open the command menu, and then click the **Toolbar** toggle option.

To switch between a window and full screen, click the Full screen toolbar icon shown to the right. The <Alt+Enter> key combination also toggles between these two modes. To quit the MS-DOS window and return to normal Windows 98 operation, click the **x** (close) button of a window, or type **exit** at the command prompt.

Using the Toolbar:

The toolbar (see below) is a very useful feature of an

MS-DOS window. You can mark text and copy it to the Windows clipboard, or paste from the clipboard. You can also carry out these functions from the Command menu, by selecting **Edit**, **Mark**, **Edit**, **Copy**, or **Edit**, **Paste**, as shown here.

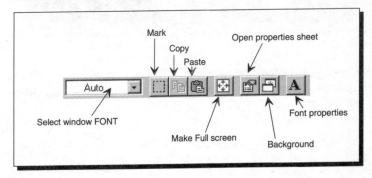

151

Using the Run Window

With Windows 98, just as in Windows 95, the easiest way to issue a single DOS command, that involves

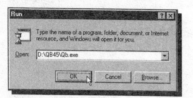

running a program, is in the **Run** window, shown here, opened from the **Start** menu. Its big advantage is that all previous commands are remembered. Clicking the down arrow, opens a small 'database' of your most used commands, including path and file names, etc. The command itself is actioned in a 'one off' DOS window, as shown below.

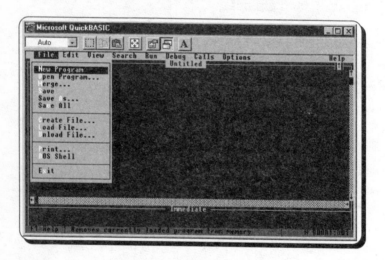

When you have finished using this window you have to close it, by clicking the **x** (close) button, in the top right hand corner of the screen.

The MS-DOS Editor

Windows 98 includes the **Edit** text editor, to be found in the \WINDOWS\COMMAND subdirectory, as shown

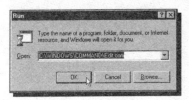

here. Users of MS-DOS will find the editor very familiar, but the version provided in both Windows 95 and 98 has several improvements over earlier versions of the program. These are:

- **Edit** is now smaller and faster.

- You can open up to nine files at the same time, split the screen between two files, and easily copy and paste information between them.

- You can open files as large as 4MB.

- You can open filenames and navigate through the directory structure just as you can in the rest of Windows.

The editor is opened, as one would expect from its name, by typing **Edit** at the command prompt.

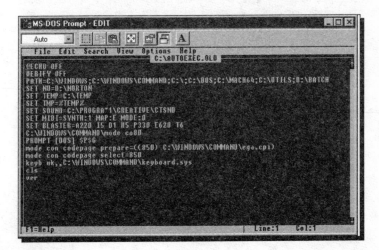

153

The file opened in the editor's window shown on the previous page, is our old **autoexec.bat** file which we renamed **autoexec.old**. As we have said earlier, we would like you to keep this file for a while, as you might want to use a shortened version later, after we introduce you to a certain topic which will be discussed shortly.

In the meantime, we will leave it up to you to explore this new addition to your MS-DOS environment. To help you on your way, the **F1** key will open a list of all the cursor movement, editing, and function commands, as well as some shortcut keys.

DOS Program Properties

With earlier versions of Windows you had to make and edit a PIF (program information file) for a particular DOS program, to control how it functioned under Windows. This procedure was not understood, or used, by many people, so most DOS programs wouldn't work properly for them under Windows.

With Windows 95 and 98, PIF files still exist, but you don't need to worry about them. They are either provided already, or made up by Windows from an existing file, or from settings you easily control, in an applications Properties sheet. Every object in Windows has a set of properties, and with MS-DOS based (rather than Windows based) programs, this sheet very strictly controls how the program will function when run in Windows.

The easy way to open an application's property sheet is to right-click the application icon in a folder and select **Properties** from the opened object menu. To demonstrate this, we will look through all the properties of the DOS program **command.com**, which is in the Windows folder and is the program run when you click the **MS-DOS Prompt** from the **Start** cascade menu.

The opening sheet, shown below, gives the file's details and allows you to set its attributes. Clicking the Program tab, opens the next sheet, shown on the next page.

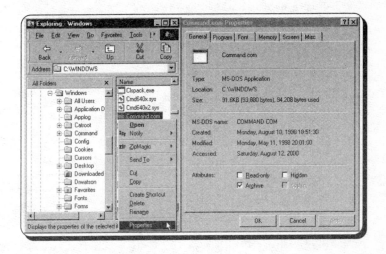

To find out more detail on any option, click the **?** window button and then click the query pointer on the item. A description box is displayed, like the one below, which opens when the **Advanced** button in the Program tab sheet, shown on the second screen dump overleaf, is clicked. The Advanced Program Settings sheet is shown on the third screen dump overleaf.

> Click this to either set up this program to have exclusive use of your computer (MS-DOS mode) or to enable Windows-based programs to be run in addition to this program.

Spending some time working through these sheets will ensure that your MS-DOS applications work the way you want them to, when run under Windows.

Problematic DOS Programs:

If you experience problems when running old DOS programs under Windows 98, such as the sudden appearance of the dreaded 'fatal exception error' on your screen, then do the following:

- If you know the name of the executable file of your DOS program, but don't know where it is on your hard disc, use the **Start, Find Files or Folders** command to locate it. Such a file should have the extension **.exe** or **.com**.

- Use the My Computer program to highlight the executable file, click the Properties button on the toolbar, and press the Program tab of the displayed Properties dialogue box. Next press the **Advanced** button to display the Advanced Program Settings dialogue box.

Click the **Prevent MS-DOS-based programs from detecting Windows** to check it and click the **OK** button twice to close the Properties dialogue boxes.

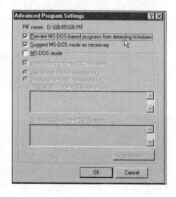

156

DOS Programs Running Procedure

To help ensure as many MS-DOS based programs as possible work properly with Windows 98, the file **apps.inf** is provided, containing program settings for many popular MS-DOS applications. These settings are based on test results and specify the special settings necessary to allow the application to run under Windows 98.

When you attempt to run an MS-DOS application, Windows first looks for its PIF. If one doesn't exist for that application, the **apps.inf** file is searched. If the application is listed, the system reads the contents and creates a PIF that is used to run the program.

To provide support for 'rogue' MS-DOS-based applications that work only under MS-DOS (requiring full access to the system components and resources), Windows 98 provides an **MS-DOS mode**. In this mode, also known as 'real mode', Windows removes itself from memory (except for a small section) and provides the application with full access to all the resources of the computer. Not many applications need to run in single MS-DOS application mode, but one of them is MSBackup, provided with MS-DOS 6.

To set up a program to run in this mode, you select **MS-DOS mode** on the Advanced Program Settings sheet (as shown at the top of the previous page) for the application. On this sheet you can also specify a **config.sys** and an **autoexec.bat** file to run for the application. When the application is then run, Windows closes all running tasks, configures the PC to use the **config.sys** and **autoexec.bat** files for the session, restarts the computer, loads a real-mode copy of MS-DOS, and runs the application.

When you close the MS-DOS application, Windows restarts as normal. This is quite a performance and if you have a slow PC it is very time consuming. However, there is a better way, which we discuss next.

Resurrecting MS-DOS 7

There might be times when it is imperative to boot up your PC in MS-DOS, particularly if you are still running DOS programs which require maximum RAM memory. Running such programs from within a Windows 98 DOS shell will most certainly cause problems.

Microsoft has tried hard to present Windows 98 as a standalone operating system, but in reality Windows 98 still sits on top of the old (cut-down) version of MS-DOS 7. DOS starts up exactly in the same way as it always did, except that its **command.com** file is customised to run the **win.com** file (to be found within the WINDOWS folder).

However, this auto-start of **win.com** can be blocked easily by changing part of the **msdos.sys** file, thus saving start-up time by eliminating the loading of the Windows bitmap banner, and booting directly in DOS.

To achieve this, do the following:

- Start your computer, then disable the Fast Shutdown facility as discussed at the end of the previous chapter. This is important and must be done first.

- Use the **Start, Shut Down** command, select **Restart in MS-DOS mode** option, as shown below, and press **OK**.

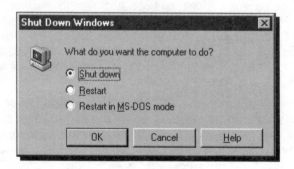

It is important that what follows is carried out after this restart option in DOS, and not by simply dropping into a DOS shell from within Windows 98.

- When the computer restarts in MS-DOS mode, it will be logged on to the WINDOWS subdirectory shown by the prompt

  ```
  C:\WINDOWS
  ```

- Change the logged directory to the root directory by typing **cd** and pressing <Enter>. Then type the following command:

  ```
  attrib -h -r -s msdos.sys
  ```

  which turns off the file's hidden, read only, and system file attributes.

- Activate the editor by typing

  ```
  edit msdos.sys
  ```

- Change the entry under the [Options] part of the displayed file from BootGUI=1 (on) to 0 (off), and add the extra line Logo=0, so that it reads as follows:

  ```
  [Options]
  BootGUI=0
  Logo=0
  ```

- Exit the editor and save your changes, then type

  ```
  attrib +h +r +s msdos.sys
  ```

  to reinstate the attributes of the file.

Just as you can boot-up in DOS 7, you can also end a session in DOS, even when using the **Shut down** Windows procedure which again saves time by not loading the two bitmap screens, which are:

```
Logow.sys
```
(the Windows logo bitmap), and
```
Logos.sys
```
(the shutdown bitmap).

All you have to do is rename these two files which are to be found in the WINDOWS directory, as follows:

- Change the logged directory from the root to the WINDOWS directory by typing **cd\windows** at the prompt and pressing <Enter>. Then type the following commands:

```
ren logow.sys logowold.sys
ren logos.sys logosold.sys
```

  we retained the original extension letters so you can remember them, should you, for some reason, want to reactivate these files later.

- Finally, type

```
exit
```

  at the prompt to exit the Windows DOS-mode and cause your computer to restart in DOS 7.

Next time you end a Windows session, remember to click the **S̲hut down** radio button of the dialogue box.

We find that it is extremely useful to be able to distinguish between shelling out in DOS from within Windows 98 or not, by displaying an appropriate DOS prompt. Being able to distinguish between the two is necessary, because in the former case you must type **exit** to return to Windows before shutting down your PC, whilst in the latter case you can just switch off.

The obvious way to do this is to include the statement

```
PROMPT [DOS] $P$G
```

within your **autoexec.bat** file, which is also needed to provide information on such things as PATH, mouse driver and keyboard configuration (if you want to use either of these in a DOS program prior to starting Windows). Use **Edit** to trim down your renamed **autoexec.old** file, or if you haven't got one, create it, then save it as **autoexec.bat** in the root directory of the (C:) drive. The contents of our file are as follows:

```
@ECHO OFF
PATH=C:\WINDOWS;C:\WINDOWS\COMMAND
SET TEMP=C:\TEMP
SET TMP=%TEMP%
PROMPT [DOS] $P$G
C:\WINDOWS\COMMAND\mouse.com
keyb uk,,C:\WINDOWS\COMMAND\keyboard.sys
cls
ver
```

Your file could be different, of course, but lines 2, 5, 6, and 7 are essential.

You also need to write a batch file (we will call it **win.bat**) to start Windows 98 and to provide an appropriate prompt when you shell out in DOS from within Windows. This file <u>must</u> be placed in the root directory of the (C:) drive and should contain the following statements:

```
@echo off
prompt [WIN] $P$G
c:\windows\WIN.COM
cd\
prompt [DOS] $P$G
```

In this way, when you first boot up your PC the PROMPT command within your **autoexec.bat** file will be executed displaying the prompt

```
[DOS] C:\>
```

Now typing **win** starts the execution of the batch file setting the prompt to

```
[WIN] C:\>
```

then resets it back to

```
[DOS] C:\>
```

once you go through the Windows shutdown procedure. In this way you will not make the mistake of switching off your computer while in a DOS shell from within Windows 98.

You may wonder why we placed the **win.bat** file in the root directory. This is because, as we have already mentioned, Windows 98 no longer needs the **autoexec.bat** and **config.sys** files. If they are not provided, it assumes certain options by default, one of which sets the path to:

```
C:\WINDOWS;C:\WINDOWS\COMMAND
```

In fact, even if you provide a path from within your **autoexec.bat** file, unless the path starts with the default option, it inserts this at the beginning of the existing PATH statement for you. The result is that you cannot place the **win.bat** file in, say a BATCH subdirectory and change the access order of directories through the PATH command in your **autoexec.bat** file. The only way of accessing **win.bat** prior to **win.com** is to place the **win.bat** file in the root directory.

Long Filenames in DOS:

Be careful when using DOS 7 to copy or rename files with long names (they can be up to 254 characters). Unlike the Explorer which can deal with long names, DOS 7 will use the first 6 letters of your long file name, then place a tilde (~) sign followed by a number. So, if you had long names such as 'Letter to John', Letter to Paul', etc., you will end up with 'Letter~1', 'Letter~2', etc., which is not much use to you as it defeats the whole idea of long names - this is true whether you have started your computer in DOS 7 or shelled out to it from within Windows 98. Apart from long names, DOS 7 can deal with everything else you would like it to do.

You can get help with DOS commands by typing the command followed by a space and the characters '/?', as follows:

```
copy /?
```

Wildcard Characters

You are probably aware of the two Wildcard characters, * and ?. When used in a command line, * can be substituted for any number of characters in a filename mask, and ? for just a single character. Thus ***.exe**, means all files with the extension of **exe**, and ***.e??** means all files with a 3 character extension beginning with **e**.

The use of the * wildcard has been extended in Windows 95 and 98, to make it more powerful when used with long filenames. You can now use more than one * in a name mask. The following is now legal in Windows:

```
Del *Jan*
```

This command would delete all the files in the current directory with 'Jan' anywhere in their name, and is not case sensitive. So be aware!

System Files and Settings

The following is a brief overview of the system files used by both Windows 95 and 98 when starting operations, and how they compare with those used by previous versions of the operating system. Most readers could quite happily ignore the next few pages, but if you are struggling to get a 'difficult' MS-DOS program (or game) to use the full facilities of your system, you might find them useful.

Original System Files:

The table overleaf, shows how **Setup** renames the old system files for the previous operating system when either Windows 95 or Windows 98 is first installed. They are thus available for possible future use, if you revert back to your previous set-up.

Original MS-DOS filename	**Renamed filename**
autoexec.bat	autoexec.dos
command.com	command.dos
config.sys	config.dos
io.sys (or ibmbio.com)	io.dos
mode.com	mode_dos.com
msdos.sys (or ibmdos.com)	msdos.dos

New System Files:

The following 'new' files are used by Windows 95 and Windows 98 (henceforth referred to as Windows).

IO.SYS - Windows uses a new system file, **io.sys**, which replaces the two MS-DOS system files (**io.sys** and **msdos.sys**). This real-mode operating system file contains the information needed to start your computer. The files, **config.sys** and **autoexec.bat** are no longer needed to start the Windows operating system (but they are kept for backward compatibility with certain applications and drivers).

The following drivers are loaded by default in **io.sys**, if these files are found on the hard disc:

himem.sys
ifshlp.sys
setver.exe
dblspace.bin or **drvspace.bin**

Most of the functions provided by the various **config.sys** file entries are now provided by default in **io.sys**, as listed below:

dos=high	
himem.sys	
ifshlp.sys	minimal file system help loaded.
setver.exe	included for compatibility reasons.
files=	default value is 60.
lastdrive=	default value is z.
buffers=	default value is 30.
stacks=	default value is 9,256.
fcbs=	default value is 4.

The values in **io.sys** cannot be edited, to override its default values, you should place an entry in the **config.sys** file with the value you want.

MSDOS.SYS - Windows **Setup** creates a hidden, read-only system file named **msdos.sys** in the root of the computer's boot drive. This file contains important paths used to locate other Windows files, and is also created for compatibility with applications that require it to be present before they can be installed. The file also supports an [Options] section, which you can add to and edit to customise the start-up process.

CONFIG.SYS - Windows has changed the method of handling the two files **config.sys** and **autoexec.bat** during system start up. Most of their previous functions are now automatically carried out using **io.sys** and the Registry.

The **config.sys** file can contain application-specific entries in addition to information stored in **io.sys**. These are processed in the order listed, after the base **config.sys** file has been read, all devices are loaded, and COMMAND.COM is running.

If you edit **config.sys** in Windows remember not to include the **smartdrv** command, as disc-caching is now built in. Also Windows includes built-in mouse support, so remove any **device=mouse.sys,** or similar, lines.

AUTOEXEC.BAT - The **autoexec.bat** is included for compatibility purposes. If your computer has such a file, each line is processed in sequence during system start up. The file can contain additional application-specific entries that are run in the sequence they are listed.

The default Windows environment includes the following, **autoexec.bat** commands:

```
tmp=c:\windows\temp
temp=c:\windows\temp
prompt=$p$g
path=c:\windows;c:\windows\command
comspec=c:\windows\command\command.com
```

If you edit the **autoexec.bat** file, remember not to include other versions of Windows in the path, not to change the MS-DOS commands directory from the path, and not to add SMARTDrive, or other disc caches. The PATH statement should always start with

```
C:\WINDOWS;C:\WINDOWS\COMMAND
```

SYSTEM.INI and WIN.INI - Most configuration options for Windows are now stored in the Registry and are no longer required in the **system.ini** and **win.ini** files.

BOOTLOG.TXT - The **bootlog.txt** file is created during **Setup** when the Windows operating system is first started, and contains a record of the current start- up process for the system. It shows the Windows components and drivers loaded and initialised, and the status of each.

If you press the **F8** function key when the words 'Starting Windows ..' first display on your screen, you can enter the option for interactive system start-up, in which you can choose to create a boot log.

The Registry

Windows 98 uses a central location, called the Registry, to store information previously held in the **.ini** files used by earlier versions of Windows.

The Registry is structured as a hierarchical database to store text or binary value information and maintains all of the configuration parameters previously stored in the three Windows system files, **win.ini**, **system.ini**, and **protocol.ini**, and other application-specific **.ini** files.

Like the **config.sys** and **autoexec.bat** files, these **.ini** files are still used for compatibility reasons. Hopefully developers of new Windows 98 applications will, in the future, use the Registry to consolidate their application-specific information.

To take a look in your Registry, type the command REGEDIT into the **Start**, **Run** text box.

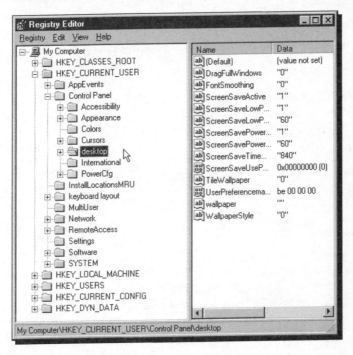

When new Plug and Play devices are installed, the system checks the existing configuration in the Registry to determine which hardware resources are not being used, so that the new device can be properly configured without conflicting with a device already installed in the system.

Note: We would not recommend you making any changes in your Registry, unless you are an expert and know precisely what you are doing.

167

INDEX

171

173

COMPANION DISCS TO BOOKS

COMPANION DISCS are available for most computer books written by the same author(s) and published by BERNARD BABANI (publishing) LTD, as listed at the front of this book (except for those marked with an asterisk). These books contain many pages of file/program listings. There is no reason why you should spend hours typing them into your computer, unless you wish to do so, or need the practice.

Please Note: There is no companion disc for this book.

ORDERING INSTRUCTIONS

To obtain companion discs, fill in the order form below, or a copy of it, enclose a cheque (payable to **P.R.M. Oliver**) or a postal order, and send it to the address given below. **Make sure you fill in your name and address** and specify the book number and title in your order.

Book No.	Book Name	Unit Price	Total Price
BP		£3.50	
BP		£3.50	
BP		£3.50	
Name		Sub-total	£............
Address		P & P (@ 45p/disc)	£............
....			
....			
		Total Due	£............

Send to: P.R.M. Oliver, CSM, Pool, Redruth, Cornwall, TR15 3SE

175

NOTES